# HOW TO GET A PhD

Managing the peaks and troughs of research

## Estelle M. Phillips
BIRKBECK COLLEGE, UNIVERSITY OF LONDON

## and

## D. S. Pugh
THE OPEN UNIVERSITY

OPEN UNIVERSITY PRESS
MILTON KEYNES : PHILADELPHIA

Open University Press
Open University Educational Enterprises Limited
12 Cofferidge Close
Stony Stratford
Milton Keynes MK11 1BY, England

*and*

242 Cherry Street
Philadelphia, PA 19106, USA

First published 1987
Reprinted 1988 (twice)

*British Library Cataloguing in Publication Data*

Phillips, Estelle
  How to get a PhD.
  1. Doctor of philosophy degree – Great Britain
  I. Title   II. Pugh, D. S.
  378'.24     LB2391.G8

  ISBN 0-335-15537-5
  ISBN 0-335-15536-7 (pbk.)

*Library of Congress Cataloging in Publication Data*

Phillips, Estelle,
  How to get a Ph.D.

  1. Doctor of philosophy degree – Great Britain.
  2. Universities and colleges – Great Britain – Graduate work.
  I. Pugh, Derek Salman.   II. Title.
  LB2386.P47  1987    378'.24'0941    87–7341
  ISBN 0-335-15537-5
  ISBN 0-335-15536-7 (pbk.)

Typeset by Scarborough Typesetting Services
Printed in Great Britain by
Thomson Litho Ltd, East Kilbride, Scotland

# HOW TO GET A PhD

Dedicated to
SHELDON, JEROME AND BRADLEY REBACK
and
THE PUGHS and THE ARIELS

# Contents

# Acknowledgements

This book has grown out of the PhD research of EMP, the study of Open University research students (EMP), the experience of supervising and examining doctoral students (DSP) and the seminar on the process of PhD-getting conducted by DSP for a number of years at the London Business School and subsequently at the Open University.

We should like to acknowledge the help of all students and supervisors who contributed to those activities over the years and who form the 'cast of characters' in this book. We learned a lot from all of them and we are most grateful.

A number of colleagues and students commented on earlier drafts of this book. We should like to thank Rachel Asch, Dr David Blackburn, Professor Sidney Greenbaum, Dr Jean Hartley, Dr Paul Long, Simon Marvin, Helena Pugh, Natalie Pugh and Martin Sullivan. Julia Tyler helpfully obtained some further information. Two anonymous reviewers for the Open University Press made a number of encouraging and useful points which we greatly appreciate.

At the Open University Systems Group the transfer of text to and from page, disc and word processor was made possible with the help of Jennie Moffat, John Naughton, Dr Sheila Stone and Dr Lewis Watson. Thank you.

Finally, our most heartfelt thanks go to Natalie Pugh for her continuous support and hospitality, which made the writing of this book, necessarily within strict deadlines, a comfortable rather than a stressful experience.

# 1

# Becoming a postgraduate

This book is a handbook and a survival manual for PhD students. If you are intending to embark on a research degree it will introduce you to the system and, by increasing your understanding, help you to improve your choice of university, polytechnic, college, department and supervisor.

If you have just picked this book up and you are already a research student, then you should read it thoroughly – and hang on to it so that you can refer to it frequently. You will need to do this because we shall be discussing the skills and processes that are crucial to obtaining the PhD degree.

If you are a supervisor, or contemplating becoming one, the book is highly relevant to you too, because it deals with the educational processes that it is your responsibility to encourage for the successful completion of your students' research degrees.

## The nature of postgraduate education

Acquiring the skills and understanding the processes necessary for success cannot be done at a single reading. As a research student you need continually to use the ideas in this book to develop your own insight into your own situation. In this way your professional learning will develop as it should – under your own management.

'Under your own management' is the key to the nature of post-graduate (and particularly doctoral) education. In undergraduate education a great deal, in academic terms, is organized for the student. It may not have seemed like that to you at the time, because you were required to do a considerable amount of work; but, for example, syllabuses were laid down, textbooks were specified, practical sessions were designed, the examinations were organized to cover a set range of topics in questions of a known form, and so on. You could quite reasonably have complained if asked about an extraneous subject: 'But no one told me that I was supposed to learn that topic (or methodology or theory or historical period).' For the most part you were following an academic course set by your teachers.

In doctoral education, *you* have to take responsibility for managing your learning and for getting yourself a PhD. Of course, there will be people around to help you – your supervisor, other academics in your department, fellow students and so on. Some of them will even tell you what, in their opinion, you have to do to obtain the degree; but the responsibility *for determining what is required*, as well as for carrying it out, remains firmly with you. And if it turns out that you need a particular topic or theory for your work, then it is no excuse to say: 'But nobody told me it was relevant.' It is your responsibility.

So you will not be traversing a set course laid out by others. You will be expected to initiate discussions, ask for the help that you need, argue about what you should be learning, and so on. You are under self-management; so it is no use sitting around waiting for somebody to tell you what to do next or, worse, complaining that nobody is telling you what to do next; in the postgraduate world these are opportunities, not deficiencies.

### The psychology of being a postgraduate

New postgraduates enter the system determined to make an outstanding contribution to their subject. By the time that they enter the final stages of thesis-writing for the degree they are determined to 'get it and forget it'! During the intervening years their enthusiasm has been dampened by the demands of having to concentrate on a specific topic and conduct routine and repetitive tasks in an atmosphere where nobody seems either to understand or to care about their work.

They come into the university or college knowing precisely who they are: successful and intelligent holders of well-earned qualifications. It is not long before they lose their initial confidence and begin to question their own self-image. This is the result of contacts (no matter how sporadic or from what distance) with academic discourse. Such contacts could come from members of staff, postgraduates who are further into their research than the first-year students, and papers published in journals or presented at conferences. These challenge the assumptions and conceptions that the young graduates had accepted as inviolable. From this period of self-doubt and questioning, the successful postgraduates emerge with a new identity as competent professionals, able to argue their viewpoint with anybody regardless of status, confident of their own knowledge but also aware of its boundaries. This new identity permits them to ask for information when they are aware that they don't know something and to express a lack of understanding when this is necessary, instead of pretending that there is no difficulty for fear of being thought stupid. To arrive at this point is what being a postgraduate research student is really all about.

## The aims of this book

The necessity for personal academic initiative is the key cultural change that doctoral students will encounter compared with their undergraduate days. It requires a different style of operation, which is why it is not sufficient just to state the issue as we did in the previous sections. Students need information and insights to develop the capacity to operate successfully in the postgraduate environment. We have seen many students take long periods (one year or even two!) in adjusting to the environment, at considerable jeopardy to the achievement of their doctorates. Some students never come to terms with it and go away indignant, bitter – and without PhDs.

All new postgraduates have to be prepared to unlearn and rethink many of the doctrines which they have had to accept up to this point in their student career. A vital aspect of this rethinking is to take the initiative in discussing with your supervisor the whole range of your ideas, including any that might even appear to be 'off-beat' or 'illegitimate' but may in fact turn out to be surprisingly useful leads.

The remainder of this book is devoted to exploring such issues in a realistic way, in order to help students understand and carry out the tasks necessary to complete their PhDs successfully. We shall be drawing on our experience in doctoral supervision and our systematic research into PhD education. We give real-life examples of students and their supervisors. These illustrations cover a range of faculties, including Arts, Science, Social Science, and Technology. The ratio of men to women is consistent with that in higher education today. We shall be examining the characteristics of the educational system, the nature of the PhD qualification, psychological aspects of the PhD process, and how to manage your supervisor, among many other practical topics.

## Action summary

1 Be aware that in doctoral education you are under your own management and have the responsibility for determining what is required as well as for carrying it out.
2 You will experience periods of self-doubt which you must come through with the clear aim of becoming a competent professional researcher.
3 Read this book for insights into the PhD research learning process, to help you manage it better.

# 2

# Getting into the system

Once you have decided to continue within the higher education system and conduct research for a higher degree, you have other decisions to make. First you have to be accepted by a university or polytechnic department to work in your chosen area of study. But which university? In what area? And how to apply?

**Choosing the institution and field of study**

If you are a postgraduate who is a candidate for a research studentship, the offer of such a studentship is likely to be the determining factor in your choice of institution and field of study. You should, though, satisfy yourself on two important counts:

(i) That the research discipline or area in which the studentship is offered is genuinely one on which you can see yourself concentrating very closely for the next three years of your life and maybe more. Many PhD students have come unstuck simply because they have lost interest or belief in the area that they are investigating.

(ii) That the university or polytechnic department in which you are being offered the studentship has an established

reputation in research and a real commitment to the development of doctoral students. You should not hesitate to ask
about these issues, so important to your success, when you
go to a department for interview. You should collect whatever literature is available about the department, the staff
engaged in research and the precise nature of that research.
Obtain copies of research papers and discover as much as
you can about the scope of existing work being done by staff
and doctoral students and the possibilities of developing that
work into areas of interest to you. Ask to speak to current
doctoral students and obtain from them a description of the
adequacy of the set-up from their point of view.

Accept a studentship only if you are optimistic on both counts –
of the suitability of the institution and of the field of study. This
optimism will fade soon enough, as we shall see later on in this
book, so it is important to have some to start off with.

If you are not dependent on a studentship (or if you are fortunate enough to be offered more than one and have to choose)
then you have a wider range of options, but you will have to
work harder to acquaint yourself with the available possibilities.

One direct way of finding out about the relevant academic
activities is to go to a university or polytechnic library and
systematically review the current issues of the journals in your
subject. This allows you to locate the researchers who are publish-
ing relevant work. Remember, all libraries in higher education
will allow readers to have access to their stock for use on the
premises – you just have to ask for permission.

It is always a good idea, once you have narrowed down your
options to a few departments that appeal to you, to contact those
who seem most likely to be able to discuss your own plans in the
light of what they know to be happening in their unit. You can
initiate this contact by letter, followed by a telephone call and – if
you are still interested – an arrangement to meet at the university
or polytechnic. You will find that most academics will be happy
to discuss research issues with you.

Having got this far your top priority should be defining more
clearly your field of study. To do this you need to give some
thought to your own interests and how they interact with what
you have found out about the work of the department you are
visiting. While it is premature, at this stage, to have a complete
project worked out, you will need to be able to talk convincingly

about the type of research that appeals to you and why you are considering applying to that particular department.

Other issues to be borne in mind at this point have to do with the mechanics of getting the work done. For example, access to laboratory equipment (and what kind of equipment?), library facilities, potential samples and their availability and ease of access, amount of support from secretarial staff (if any), photocopying facilities and, in the case of survey research, the potential for help with postage, etc. In addition, the compatibility of the people with whom you will be working is an important component in your choice.

If you are contemplating part-time doctoral research, or are otherwise subject to geographical constraints in your choice, remember that nowadays most regions have several institutions of higher learning where research degrees can be taken. For example, in the West Midlands conurbation there are at least three universities and three polytechnics. You should also consider that you can do a PhD under the Open University system, which has considerable geographical flexibility. For these reasons you must explore thoroughly the range of provision in your area.

## Choosing your work context

An important aspect of the quality of your working life as a research student is your work context. *Where* precisely will you be spending most of your time in the next few years? If you are in a position to make a choice of research institutions, you should certainly find out about the physical facilities offered and take them into account.

Some universities provide study cubicles for postgraduates, some a student common room and some give their research students a desk in a small shared room similar to those used by members of staff. Others make little or no provision for postgraduates. They are expected to work at home when not in libraries, laboratories, other organizations or away on field trips.

It may be that you prefer the congenial company of others in a similar situation and like the idea of being able to find a corner in a large room set aside solely for the use of research students. On the other hand, you may find it irritating having to interact with others and listen to what they have to say about their own progress (or lack of it) whenever you want to use the common room as a base from which to get on with your own work.

Perhaps you are a loner and enjoy the discipline of long hours spent poring over books or documents when not engaged in experimentation or other forms of data collection. You favour a clear dividing line between working hours and time spent socializing and are able to organize this division of activity satisfactorily yourself. Once again, you may discover that the isolation this type of work context imposes on you results in feelings of alienation and a lack of contact with others who could stimulate discussion and collaborate in the production of new ideas.

Some people believe that being given a desk in a room shared by only one or two other research students is an ideal arrangement. They have their own personal corner where they can keep their books and writing materials, interview others and chat with their room mates, as well as having easy and constant access to their supervisors and other members of staff. However, the reality is not always like that, and you may find that you are thrown into close contact with people whom you find quite intolerable for some reason or other. Perhaps one of them never stops smoking, while another is constantly talking or entertaining friends when you wish to concentrate on your work. One is very untidy and continually 'borrows' your possessions without returning them, as well as spreading items that do not belong to you all over your designated work area. Another is intrusive in other ways: perhaps there are too many questions about your personal life or too much discussion of others' problems and successes.

In addition, your presence and absence are easily noted by others, and you may have to account for your movements rather more than you would wish. Also, your supervisor 'just along the corridor' may not be quite as accessible as at first appears.

## Selecting your supervisor

This is probably the most important step you will have to take. In general students do not select their supervisors: their supervisors are allocated by the department or, in fewer cases, their supervisors may have selected them.

However, it is not impossible to influence the selection yourself and you should certainly attempt to do so. There is certain basic information that you need in order to be confident that a particular academic is an appropriate person to supervise you. The key factor is whether the academic has an established research record and is continuing to contribute to the development of his or her discipline. The questions you need to ask include the following: Have they published research papers recently? Do they hold research grants or contracts? Are they invited to speak at conferences in Britain and abroad? Positive answers to at least some of these questions are desirable.

Another important aspect that you should be considering when selecting your supervisor is: how close a relationship do you want? The supervisor–student relationship is one of the closest that you will ever be involved in. Even marriage partners do not spend long hours every day in close contact with each other, but this could be the case with a student and a supervisor. Some people need to have their supervisors around a lot (especially in the beginning), while others feel it oppressive to be asked what they are doing, and to be told continually what they should be getting on with next.

There are at least two patterns from which to choose with regard to working with your supervisor. The first has already been mentioned: the student needs constant support and re-assurance, and the supervisor needs continual feedback in order to give instruction, thus providing direction for the research. The second pattern is a relationship in which the student needs time to think about the work to be done and needs the freedom to make mistakes during early attempts to get started, before discussing what has been happening with the supervisor. In this relationship the supervisor must feel relaxed about giving the student time to learn by trial and error. Such supervisors are content to give guidance at regular intervals rather than the direction provided by those who stay much closer to the students and their work.

Research has shown (Phillips 1979) that when a student who needs time to plan work and to continue unhurriedly until satisfied that there is something interesting to impart is paired with a supervisor who constantly asks for worthwhile results, the student becomes irritated and feels that the standards required are unattainable. The supervisor feels that the post-graduate is too cautious and unable to work alone. Conversely, when a student who needs constant feedback and encouragement is paired with a supervisor who wants to be kept informed of progress and ideas only at intervals that allow for some development to have occurred, the student feels neglected and the supervisor resents the student's demands for attention (if the student is actually confident enough to ask for more time).

It seems that 'rapport' and good communication between students and their supervisors are the most important elements of supervision. Once the personal relationship has been well established, all else falls into place. If interpersonal compatibility is missing everything else to do with being a postgraduate is perceived negatively. Therefore, it cannot be too strongly stressed that discussion of this relationship should begin at the very earliest opportunity, and a tentative agreement about working together should be reached.

## Becoming a research student

In general very little is done in the way of induction into the higher degree system or into the role of postgraduate student. Those who have recently attained a high-quality first degree share with their peers who have returned to university after some years of working the confusion and disorientation that comes from not quite knowing what is expected of them.

Often, new research students have the idea that people who possess a PhD degree are outstandingly brilliant. This idea inhibits their own development as they are equally sure that they are not outstandingly brilliant and, therefore, cannot really expect to be awarded a PhD. Similarly, if they actually read any completed theses (this is not the norm and will be discussed in detail later) they often emerge convinced that they would never be able to write anything even remotely resembling such a document either in length or quality.

Wason (1974) described the 'ill-defined limbo' which he saw the world of the postgraduate as, and spoke of the traumatic intellectual transition which had to be made, during which new students might question the whole point of their being in the university. While the graduate system in America is different in many ways from that in Britain, Vartuli (1982) clearly documented there the phenomenon of 'unlearning existing expertise' and having to start from the very beginning of the unknown in order to discover slowly what one is supposed to be doing. She is describing how it felt to become a research student from a woman's point of view, but the experiences of men are not dissimilar, according to Wason (1974) and Phillips (1979).

The new research student should, therefore, make every effort to avoid these unpleasant beginnings by agreeing a small initial project with definite deadlines at an early interview with the supervisor. The agreement should include the understanding that, once the work has been completed, the supervisor and student will discuss both the work itself *and* the student's feelings about it. This exercise will help to clarify any doubts about the student's ability to undertake research and written work. It will also help to reveal the evolutionary process (corrections, drafts, rewritings, etc.) inevitably involved in the production of theses, articles and books to publication standard – the like of which the student has just read with such admiration.

It is also a good idea to talk to other postgraduates about their experience of the role as well as their work. Sharing apprehensions helps to resolve them through the knowledge that the problem is not an individual one, but one that is inbuilt into a less than perfect system.

## Myths and realities of the system

### The 'ivory tower'

One of the commonest misconceptions about research is that it is an 'ivory tower' activity, far removed from reality and from social contact with others. If you say you are doing research, people will often talk to you as though you had decided to spend a number of years in solitary confinement from which, in due course, you will emerge with your new discoveries.

It is not like that at all. Although there are considerable periods when you will be working on your own (thinking and writing, for example) this is not the whole story. There is also a considerable academic network of people with whom, as an active researcher, you must interact. These include your supervisor, other academics in your department, the general library staff, the specialist librarian who deals with computer-based literature searches, visiting academics giving seminars, colleagues giving papers at conferences – the list is very considerable. To be an effective research student you must make use of all the opportunities offered. Research is an interactive process and requires the development of social, as well as academic, skills.

### Personal relationships

Wason (1974) noted the effort that it took new research students to address their supervisors by their first names. Yet most supervisors feel that so long as they *are* on first-name terms with their research students everything is fine and the student knows that they are friends. Some supervisors even invite their students to their homes or take them to the pub for a drink in order to reinforce this camaraderie. But no matter how far the supervisors may go to assure their new students that their relationship is to be that of friendly colleagues, the students take a considerable amount of time to become comfortable about this degree of informality. This is as true of mature students as of the more usual new graduate.

The reason for the students' difficulty is that the supervisors already have that which the students most want – the PhD. They have the title of 'Dr' and are acknowledged experts in the chosen field of their research students. The students have admired the supervisors' work during their undergraduate days, having come into contact with it through lectures or reading, or having heard reference made to it by others. They feel privileged to be working so closely with such an individual, and are aware of the supervisor's authority in the subject and power in the relationship.·

So far as interaction with peers is concerned, students seem to have some difficulty. This is more usually to do with the structure of postgraduate departments and the system of education at this level than with anything of a more personal nature. The system lacks organized seminars for postgraduates, and a minimum of thought is given to the task of helping to establish links between them. The reality of the situation is that personal relationships within the academic community, as elsewhere, have to be worked at and take time to develop.

## Teamworking

'I work alone in a lab. full of people, all research students, all working alone.' This quotation is from Diana, a student in biochemistry, who was part of a 'team' of postgraduate students who were all engaged in the search for an effective anti-cancer drug. It exemplifies the situation in scientific research, in which a large programme is being funded and the professors who hold the grants gather around them several research students. Each student is working on a specific problem. Each problem is closely linked to all the others. In theory there is a free exchange of information and the whole group works in harmony. In many programmes though postgraduates take care to guard closely the work for which they are responsible because they are all in constant fear that one of the others will discover something that will render their own research unworthy of continuation.

The PhD is awarded for original work. Postgraduates working on a programme such as the one described have two worries: first, that another student's work so closely borders on their own that it will make their work 'unoriginal' or second past the post; second, that somebody else will demonstrate something (for which that other person will be awarded a PhD) that will at the same time show *their* line of research to be false.

What is needed is collaboration, not competition, between people who should be making each other's work more comprehensible and less alienating. Yet so many students experience alienation and isolation as the overriding themes of their postgraduate days. The strange thing about this is that the science students appear to feel the isolation more strongly than their counterparts in the social sciences or arts faculties. This is because within the sciences there is the illusion of companionship and the expectations of new postgraduates are that they will be part of a group of friends, as well as a work group. We have already seen that this is not necessarily so.

In other faculties new postgraduates expect to be working alone in libraries or at home, reading, writing and thinking rather than experimenting. Any socializing that may take place as a result of a seminar, shared room or organized event is perceived as a bonus.

### 'Scientific method'

'Hypotheses,' said Medawar in 1964, 'are imaginative and inspirational in character'; they are 'adventures of the mind'. He was arguing in favour of the position taken by Karl Popper in *The Logic of Scientific Discovery* (1972) that the nature of scientific method is hypothetico-deductive and not, as is generally believed, inductive.

It is essential that you, as an intending researcher, understand the difference between these two interpretations of the research process so that you do not become discouraged or begin to suffer from a feeling of 'cheating' or not going about it the right way.

The myth of scientific method is that it is inductive: that the formulation of scientific theory starts with the basic, raw evidence of the senses – simple, unbiased, unprejudiced observation. Out of these sensory data – commonly referred to as 'facts' – generalizations will form. The myth is that from a disorderly array of factual information an orderly, relevant theory will somehow emerge. However, the starting point of induction is an impossible one.

There is no such thing as unbiased observation. Every act of observation we make is a function of what we have seen or otherwise experienced in the past. All scientific work of an experimental or exploratory nature starts with some expectation about the outcome. This expectation is an hypothesis. They provide the initiative and incentive for the inquiry and influence the method. It is in the light of an expectation that some observations are held to be relevant and some irrelevant, that one methodology is chosen and others discarded, that some experiments are conducted and others are not. Where is your naive, pure and objective researcher now?

Hypotheses arise by guesswork, or by inspiration, but having been formulated they can and must be tested rigorously, using the appropriate methodology. If the predictions you make as a result of deducing certain consequences from your hypothesis are not shown to be correct then you must discard or modify your hypothesis. If the predictions turn out to be correct then your hypothesis has been supported and may be retained until such time as some further test shows it not to be correct. Once you have arrived at your hypothesis, which is a product of your imagination, you then proceed to a strictly logical and rigorous process, based upon deductive argument – hence the term 'hypothetico-deductive'.

So don't worry if you have some idea of what your results will tell you before you even begin to collect data; there are no scientists in existence who really wait until they have all the evidence in front of them before they try to work out what it might possibly mean. The closest we ever get to this situation is when something happens serendipitously; but even then the researcher has to formulate a hypothesis to be tested before being sure that, for example, a mould might prove to be a successful antidote to bacterial infection.

The myth of scientific method is not only that it is inductive (which we have seen is incorrect) but also that the hypothetico-deductive method proceeds in a step-by-step, inevitable fashion. The hypothetico-deductive method describes the *logical* approach to much research work, but it does not describe the *psychological* behaviour that brings it about. This is much more holistic – involving guesses, reworkings, corrections, blind alleys and above all inspiration, in the deductive as well as the hypothetic component – than is immediately apparent from reading the final thesis or published papers. These have been, quite properly, organized into a more serial, logical order so that the worth of the *output* may be evaluated independently of the behavioural process by which it was obtained. It is the difference, for example, between the academic papers with which Crick and Watson demonstrated the structure of the DNA molecule, and the fascinating book *The Double Helix* in which Watson (1968) described how they did it. From this point of view, 'scientific method' may more usefully be thought of as a way of *writing up* research rather than as a way of carrying it out.

**Action summary**

1 Get as much information as you can before choosing your academic institution. Visit the places beforehand and talk to potential supervisors. Ask to see around the area in which your work will be carried out to determine whether it would suit you.
2 Find out about a potential supervisor's research experience, published record and supervisory management style before making your decision.
3 Very early on, arrange with your supervisor to carry out a small initial project with definite deadlines, to get you into the system. On completion and writing up, discuss not only the results but also how you went about it and what you can learn about the process.
4 Work at personal relationships with your supervisor and fellow doctoral students. Set limited goals and achieve them.
5 Find out from researchers in your subject how the scientific approach actually works in practice.

# 3

# The nature of the PhD qualification

In this chapter we shall discuss the nature of a PhD. We shall consider the objectives of the process, the part that it plays in the academic system, and the inevitably different aims the students, the supervisors and the examiners bring to it.

## The meaning of a doctorate

We are going to start with some historical background and present in a schematic way the meaning of the degree structure of a British university.

- A bachelor's degree traditionally meant that the recipient had obtained a *general* education (specializing at this level is a relatively recent 19th-century development).
- A master's degree is a licence to practise. Originally this meant to practise theology, i.e. to take a living in the Church, but now there are master's degrees across the whole range of disciplines: business administration, soil biology, computing, applied linguistics and so on. The degree marks the possession of advanced knowledge in a specialist field.

- A doctor's degree is a licence to teach – meaning to teach in a university as a member of a faculty. This does not mean now-adays that becoming a lecturer is the only reason for taking a doctorate, since the degree has much wider career conno-tations outside academia and many PhDs do not have aca-demic teaching posts. The concept stems, though, from the need for a faculty member to be an authority, in full command of the subject right up to the boundaries of current knowledge, and able to extend them.

There are a number of exceptions to these descriptions of the meaning of the degree titles, since British universities pride themselves on their independence; there are, for example, no laws that specify which degrees can be awarded, by which insti-tutions, to whom and on what basis, as is the case in Continental countries.

Thus the arts faculties of traditional Scottish universities use the MA title for their first degree, but the science faculties use BSc. Traditionally there was no extra examination for an MA degree at Oxford and Cambridge, only a requirement to continue attendance at a college for a further two years. In modern times this has been reduced to paying a registration fee after two years and obtaining the degree even without attendance.

In medicine the practice is even stranger: general medical prac-titioners are given the honorary title of Doctor although they do not have a doctorate from their universities. Indeed, on the basis of their university course they are credited with *two* bachelor's degrees, although having a licence to practise they exemplify the concept of a master's degree. There are, of course, good histori-cal reasons for these anomalies.

The concept of a university doctorate has always been clear. As the highest degree that can be awarded, it proclaims that the recipient is worthy of being listened to *as an equal* by the appro-priate university faculty. Traditionally the doctorates of British universities have been named for the particular faculty; for example: DD (Divinity), MD (Medicine), LL D (Law), DMus (Music). In fact in British universities the PhD degree is a com-paratively recent concept – an early 20th-century import from America. It represents a more restricted achievement than the so-called 'higher' doctorates – i.e., those given above plus the more modern ones of DSc (Science), DLitt (Letters i.e. Arts), DSocSc (Social Sciences), etc., since it envisages a limited amount of academic work (three years or so). But it still embodies the concept that the holder of the PhD is in command of the field of study and can make a worthwhile contribution to it.

## Becoming a full professional

Thus the holder of a doctorate is someone who is recognized as an authority by the appropriate faculty. In modern terms it is useful to think of this as becoming a full professional in your field. Let us try to spell out what becoming a full professional means:

- First, at the most basic level it means that you have something to say that your peers want to listen to.
- Secondly, in order to do this you must have a command of what is happening in your subject so that you can evaluate the worth of what others are doing.
- Thirdly, you must have the astuteness to discover where you can make a useful contribution.
- Fourthly, you must have mastery of appropriate techniques that are currently being used, and also be aware of their limitations.
- Fifthly, you must be able to communicate your results effectively in the professional arena.
- Sixthly, all this must be carried out in an international context; your professional peer group is worldwide. (It always was, of course, but the rate of diffusion is infinitely faster than it used to be.) You must be aware of what is being discovered, argued about, written and published by your academic community across the world.

This list clearly represents quite a tall order; not least because, as you will have spotted, most of the list concerns the learning of skills, not knowledge. The crucial distinction is between 'knowing that' and 'knowing how', as the philosopher Gilbert Ryle put it. It is not enough for someone to *tell* you that this is a fruitful area for study; that this technique is available for use; that you should write a clear paper communicating your contribution. You have to be able to carve out a researchable topic, to master the techniques required and put them to appropriate use, to communicate cogently your findings.

So there are craft skills involved in becoming a full professional, which, like any skills, have to be learned by doing the task in practice situations under supervision. The skills required cannot easily be stated by other professionals, though many aspects can be learned from them – some consciously, others unconsciously. But there have to be the twin elements of exploration and practice, which are basic to all learning of skills. This is why the PhD takes time.

As though this were not enough, there is a further complication. When you are doing a PhD, you are playing in a game *where the goalposts are continually being moved*! Obviously, what is good professional practice today may tomorrow be inadequate. What is a reasonable contribution to a new topic now might be old hat by next year. So a final and crucial skill which professionals must acquire is the ability to evaluate and re-evaluate their own work and that of others in the light of current developments. They need to be able to grow with their discipline.

It is these skills which you are trying to acquire when you embark on a PhD, and the purpose of the exercise is to become a full professional and to be able to demonstrate that you are one. It is important to keep this *professional* concept in mind because it orientates everything that you have to do. For example, you are not doing research in order to do research; you are doing research in order to demonstrate that you have learned *how* to do research to fully professional standards. (More about the implications of this later in this chapter.)

Or again, you are not writing a review of your field of study because that would be an interesting thing to do, or because 'everybody does one' (although both of these may be true). You are writing a review because it gives you an opportunity to demonstrate that you have learned how to take command of the material with the maturity and grasp of the full professional. (More about this in Chapter 6 on the form of a PhD thesis.)

Notice that the key concept is to demonstrate that your learning is to professional standards. How will you know whether it is? Well, this is probably the most crucial thing that you have to learn – from your supervisor and from published work in your field. It is indeed a vital responsibility of your supervisor to ensure that you are given every opportunity to become familiar with appropriate professional standards. It is only through this familiarity that you will be able to recognize and achieve them.

One thing is clear: you cannot get a PhD unless you do know what the standards are. This is because of the aims of the whole doctoral process. These are not just to allow you, in due course, to have the title 'Doctor' pleasant though this is and proud though your family will be. When the examiners, on behalf of the university and the academic community, award the degree and recognize you as a full professional, what they are primarily concerned with is that you should 'join the club' and continue your contribution to developing your discipline through research and scholarship throughout your career. Therefore they give you, in principle, the status *to examine other people's PhD theses*. Not immediately, of course. You will have to publish papers from your doctoral thesis and continue to research and publish in the field to establish your academic authority.

This is in fact the aim of the whole exercise: to get you to the level where you can examine others' PhDs with authority. Thus clearly you must have the professional skills and you must know the standards that are required. Two immediate corollaries of this fact are:

– Quite early on in the process you must begin to read other PhD theses in your field so that you can discover what the standards are. How else will you know what standard you ought to aim for?

– If you have to go along to your supervisor after you have done your work and ask if it is good enough, you are clearly not ready for a PhD, which is awarded as a recognition that you are able to evaluate research work (including your own) to fully professional standards.

### Aims of students

There are many reasons why people decide to work towards a PhD. One of the most common aims at the beginning is the wish to make a significant contribution to the chosen field. In these cases students have become particularly interested in a topic during the course of their undergraduate degrees (or perhaps while working in their profession) and wish to add something to the current state of knowledge. For example, Adam who, after graduating in architecture, had spent some years both teaching and working as an architect, explained why he had returned to university in the following way:

> I wanted to do more theoretical work as my interests were with the value problems in designing a building. How does the architect make decisions about features that will affect the behaviour of those using the building without ever having a consultation with the prospective users? This interest was an extension of my direction as an under-graduate and my observations during my working career. I saw it as a serious problem and a major issue in professional practice.

Greg, a history student, said he wanted to gain a PhD because:

It was an opportunity to continue research I had started for my MA. To me a PhD means that the candidate has made some new contribution to his field and that's really what I want to do. Up until now I've never really considered doing the next degree until I had almost finished the previous one. I don't need the PhD for my work – it might even be a disadvantage.

Greg's sentiments are not echoed by all research students, as another important aim for many postgraduates is to enhance career opportunities and future earning capacity through possession of the PhD degree. Some decide on this course of action when considering plans for the future; others, like Freddy who was studying industrial chemistry, decide on research when they find it more difficult than they had expected to get a job straight from university:

I wanted to work in Finland, where my girlfriend lives, and was offered two jobs, but I couldn't get a work permit. Then I started to look for work over here but by that time I was too late for any jobs that were half worthwhile. The head of department where I did my first degree offered me a research post, so I agreed after he gave me an outline of the research area.

Some students find that they are being called 'Dr' by people coming in to the laboratory or hospital department where they work and feel guilty at accepting the title they have not yet achieved. Others feel that relationships with their medical colleagues may be easier if they, too, have the title. Related to this is the situation of those women postgraduates who are doing the higher degree partly to solve the 'Miss', 'Mrs', 'Ms' problem by having the title of 'Dr'.

Another reason for undertaking a research degree is *not* having any real aims and not being able to think of anything else to do. All of this is far removed from the idealistic view of the PhD student as somebody dedicated to advancing knowledge and potentially worthy of becoming an undisputed expert in a given field.

But these diverse aims of students do not remain the same throughout the period of registration for the higher degree, not even for those students who *do* start because of the intrinsic satisfaction of actually doing research and because of their interest in the work for its own sake. The following description of his decision to work for the PhD was given by Bradley, who was studying in the English department of a university:

> I couldn't think of a more fulfilling or pleasurable way of spending my time. It's almost instinctive. I haven't weighed up the pros and cons, it was an emotional decision really.

All these students, together with very many more enthusiastic new recruits, change their way of talking about their PhD as the years of learning to do research and become a full professional pass by. Towards the end their aims become narrower: simply to reach the goal of the PhD – 'got to get it' – or else to complete an unfinished task – 'must finish'.

It is important that postgraduates eventually realize that it is determination and application, rather than brilliance, that are needed. The sooner you learn this the better. Conducting a piece of research to a successful conclusion is a job of work that has to be done just like any other job of work. Also, just like any other job of work, an important objective should be to make a success of what you have set out to do.

### Aims of supervisors

In the same way that students start to do a PhD for a variety of different reasons, so too do supervisors undertake supervision with different aims in mind. There are those who wish to add to their reputation for having a large number of successful research students of high calibre. With each additional success their own professional status is raised. Of course, the converse is also true: it is possible for academics to go down in the estimation of their peers by having a succession of students who drop out, do work of poor quality or take an exceptional amount of time to complete their theses. But those supervisors who have one or more ex-research students who are now professors speak of the achievements of these postgraduates as though they were their own.

There are at least two kinds of supervisors. Some supervisors believe that postgraduates should be encouraged to become autonomous researchers. Others believe they should be encouraged to become extremely efficient research assistants. Some supervisors have not really thought about this matter specifically but nevertheless treat their postgraduate students in such a way that it is relatively simple to deduce which implicit theory of postgraduate education and training they hold.

Some supervisors are dedicated to developing their favoured area of research by having several people exploring different, but related, problems. These people aim to build centres of excellence around themselves, which will attract visiting academics from other universities and other countries. In this way they are able to spend some time discussing their work with other specialists. They may also be able to arrange an occasional seminar given by a well-known expert. Students of these academics are likely to find that they are given small, well defined problems that closely border the research problems being pursued by other postgraduates attached to their supervisor.

There are also those few senior academics who aim to become eligible for a Nobel prize or other senior honour. What this means for their students is that they will be treated as research assistants and expected to do the work set out for them by the professor, in the limited manner of a subordinate.

As well as those who wish to get the work done as speedily and efficiently as possible, there are those supervisors who are genuinely interested in producing more and better researchers. They are prepared to offer a service of supervision to postgraduate students in the same way as they offer a service of teaching to undergraduate students. What this means for students is that they will be expected to develop their own topics for research and to operate in a more individual manner. This approach gives more autonomy but entails a more restricted academic peer group.

Thus supervisors have many different reasons for agreeing to add to work already being undertaken by engaging in the supervision of research students. Not all of these aims are mutually exclusive. But it is necessary for students to discover which approach a prospective supervisor favours in order to evaluate the implications for what will be expected of them.

It is also important for incoming postgraduates to be clear whether they wish to become autonomous researchers or superior research assistants, as well as for supervisors to become aware of which type of postgraduate is best suited to help them further their own aims.

Of course, we realize that it will be difficult for a beginning research student to understand fully the implications of this discussion. It will be even more difficult to act on such considerations. Two things that you could do are: talk to other research students in the department about their experience of supervision; and introduce into the preliminary discussions with any potential supervisor an exploration of their preferred way of working with their students.

## Aims of examiners

External examiners are academics from universities other than your own who are used to ensure that, within a given discipline, standards of quality for which the PhD degree is awarded are uniform across universities and polytechnics. Some examiners see the aims of the PhD to be a training for a career in research; some as an introduction to writing books; some as preparation for the academic life; and some, as we have suggested, to become a fully rounded professional.

Whether examiners are more interested in the research, the thesis or the performance of the candidate in the oral examination, they are looking for a command of the subject area (or context) of the research, as well as the specific topic. The British PhD is awarded for an original contribution to knowledge. So, although originality has never been adequately defined, examiners need to be satisfied that the work has a degree of originality and that it is the unaided work of the candidate.

Some suggestions for ways in which students may be considered to have shown originality have been put forward by Francis (1976), a professor of hydraulics working in the area of civil and mechanical engineering. These are by:

● setting down a major piece of new information in writing for the first time;
● giving a good exposition of another's work;
● continuing a previously original piece of work;
● carrying out original work designed by the supervisor;
● providing a single original technique, observation, or result in an otherwise unoriginal but competent piece of research;
● having followed instructions and understood the original concepts;
● having many original ideas, methods and interpretations, but the 'donkey work' (experiments, fieldwork or computations) has been performed by others under the direction of the postgraduate;
● showing originality in testing somebody else's idea.

He concludes that the examiner's interpretations of this ambiguity is an important component in the decision whether or not to award the PhD degree.

Examiners acquire reputations for their performance in this role. Some become known as difficult to please while others are prepared to take the supervisor's evaluation of the work almost without question. Some examiners make the oral examination a real test of professional knowledge and exposition, while others allow it to be more of a relaxed conversation between friends. Eventually, as a result of these reputations, they are selected to examine candidates whom the supervisor believes to be suited to the particular style of a given examiner. In this way, some candidates find that their external examiners have been chosen on the basis of how highly their supervisors regard their work. If the supervisor thinks that a particular student will only just satisfy requirements, a less exacting examiner is chosen. If, on the other hand, the supervisor considers the student's work to be of considerable merit, a 'tough' examiner is chosen; the student then has the advantage of being passed by somebody who adds prestige to the new PhD's success.

## Aims of universities and research councils

The government funded research councils that lie behind those magic initials SERC, NERC, ESRC, AFRC, and so on, provide studentships for British full-time doctoral students, as does the British Academy for arts students. In the past they took a fairly relaxed view in evaluating what happened after the studentship had been awarded, considering that this was a matter for the academic discretion of the particular department and supervisor involved. This is no longer the case.

The commonest way of not succeeding is to drop out. Very few people actually fail. The high drop-out rate of students has led the councils to demonstrate great concern about the effectiveness of their 'investment' in doctoral education. They are now putting very great pressure on universities and polytechnics to improve their completion rates.

The most public stance on this has been adopted by the Economic and Social Research Council, since it appeared to have the largest problem. In 1985 the ESRC announced that it was removing from the list of academic institutions which were eligible for awards those universities and colleges in which less than 10 per cent of ESRC-supported students submitted their theses for examination within four years. Although this may seem a very modest criterion (after all, up to 90 per cent of students were still allowed to take more than four years) nine institutions were sanctioned in this way. Such places are allowed to apply for review after a period of years, when they must demonstrate that their submission rates have been greatly improved. In 1987 the requirement was raised to 25 per cent submission within four years, and in 1989 it was due to be raised to 40 per cent. On present rates of submission that would mean that well over half of all universities and polytechnics would be taken off the supported list.

Obviously such a draconian policy has aroused a great deal of controversy in academic institutions. But the ESRC claims that its policy is justified and working. For students who started in 1980, the four-year completion rate over all universities and colleges was 25 per cent; for the 1982 starters the four-year completion rate rose to 39 per cent. Other research councils, while not making it so public, have for some years been taking completion rates into account in the award of their studentships to particular departments.

The effect of these policies has been to make academic institutions put much more effort into controlling the PhD process. They have been setting up working parties to review their supervisory practices, examine the benefits of doctoral programmes, strengthen the procedures for monitoring the progress of research students, and so on. Academics with overall departmental responsibility for doctoral students are being appointed. This book itself, and the seminars on which it is based, are illustrations of current interest in this topic.

The aim of research councils is to get a high proportion of doctoral students to complete within three or four years, and the universities and polytechnics are trying to bring this about. From the student's point of view the positive effects are that much more interest and care are being devoted to making the process work efficiently, and you should make sure that you get the benefits of these developments. A possible negative effect is that you may be forced to take a narrower view of your research than you might like in order to complete it within the stated time. Always remember, though, that there will be opportunities for further research on related issues after you have got your PhD.

## Mismatches and problems

Once we begin to see where the aims of the different groups involved with the PhD are not congruent, it is not too big a step to realize that certain conflicts are inherent in the system. For example, where a student who wishes to develop an area of research and make a significant contribution to it is paired with a supervisor who is more interested in speedy problem-solving, both of them will inevitably feel frustrated before very long. This is also true when the student's and supervisor's priorities are the other way around. Such was the case of Freddy and Professor Forsdike:

> I intend to tell the Prof. that he has to have very good justification for my working after the 31st March. It has to be something vital and important. All the poisoning work was never in the original project outline and most of the additional experimental work he gives me is quite irrelevant to my thesis.

Here the supervisor is encouraging the student to go beyond the boundaries of his thesis problem and pursue the leads that result from the original experiments. The student, however, wants no more than to complete a bounded series of experiments and write them up for a PhD.

If a supervisor is interested in discussing new ideas and exploring untested areas but is responsible merely for ensuring that the student completes a thesis of the required standard in a reasonable amount of time, the work of supervision becomes less than satisfying. Mrs Briggs, a supervisor in the arts faculty of a university, said:

> I think, generally speaking, that doing a PhD in English is a valueless occupation. If you can write you should write a book; a thesis is a bad preparation for that. Three years' concentration on problems that don't exist but need to be created is worthless training to be a university teacher. A PhD is a preparation only for academic life, a taught MA would be much better. I don't think anybody ever consults a thesis in English once it has been written; what use is that?

This supervisor was disenchanted with the university's perception of what a PhD meant, but was very much enjoying supervising a postgraduate of whom she said:

> He's always telling me things I don't know and that's exciting – except, of course, I can't know whether the things he's telling me are accurate. I try to make up to him for not being an ideal supervisor by giving him enthusiasm. He knows I think that he's interesting. I don't want to let him

down – he's such a very good research student. I introduce him to others in the field who *are* experts, and then he can approach them at any time he wishes for more specialist knowledge. He should finish the PhD in three years. He says it's a life work, and I agree that it could easily be, but the PhD is not a life work and he must finish it quickly.

Both these cases show the kinds of juggling that have to occur between defining the boundaries of the research and managing the time available for writing the thesis. Whether it is the student or the supervisor who takes the major responsibility for this does not alter the fact that decisions regarding what is appropriate, relevant and necessary have to be made throughout the student's period of registration.

**Action summary**

1 Set out to discover the standards and achievements for a full professional in your discipline that justify the award of the PhD degree.
2 Read others PhD theses in your field and evaluate them for the degree of originality in the research which has satisfied the examiners.
3 Be aware that the initial enthusiasm for the research will inevitably decline eventually. Provide the determination and application (rather than brilliance) that are required to complete the work and obtain the degree.
4 Use the completion pressures to which the research councils are subjecting universities and polytechnics to ensure that you have proper support in your studies.
5 The tension between the boundaries of the research project and the time available to complete it should be continually reviewed and adjusted by the student and the supervisor.

# 4

# How *not* to get a PhD

We want now to examine some very well established ways of *not* getting a PhD. While most examples in this chapter are drawn from Business Studies, in our experience, these tried and tested ways of failing apply to all fields and have to be pondered continually by research students. You have to be clear what your position is on each of the seven ways of failing that we shall discuss if you are not to fall foul of the traps they offer. And as we shall see, just to have them pointed out to you is not enough to avoid them. Most offer real blandishments that have to be determinedly resisted.

## Not wanting a PhD

The first method of not getting a PhD is not to *want* a PhD. This may seem very strange, considering that a student is likely to be 'starving in a garret', living on a studentship pittance, perhaps having given up a job in order to study, or relying on the earnings of a spouse to put them through the course. At the very least, you will be devoting a great deal of time and effort and energy to research. Surely, you might say, considering what I am giving up to the project, can there be any doubt that I really want a PhD?

Well, strangely enough, there can be. We think an analogy would help here. It is the case, isn't it, that none of us, research students and research supervisors, want to become millionaires? We should quite like it if someone *gave* us a million pounds and we didn't have to do anything for it – that would sound like a good idea. But we don't want to *set out* to become millionaires. Obviously we don't; otherwise we wouldn't be considering how to do research and get PhDs – we would be considering how to build a better mousetrap, how to play the property market in South East Asia, how to write a book with talking animals. . . . There are many ways of making a million pounds, but doing a PhD is not likely to be one of them.

Exactly the same phenomenon occurs in regard to PhDs. People think it would be a nice idea to do a PhD, they come with views of what they want to do and then they turn round and say: 'Please can I have a PhD for it?' And the answer is often 'No'. PhDs are given for a particular form of research activity (which we shall discuss in Chapters 5 and 6) and if you do not wish to carry out this form of work then you effectively do not *want* to do a PhD. It is precisely the same distinction as that between hoping to become a millionaire and setting out to make a million pounds.

Clearly the purpose of this book is to help you to set out to obtain a PhD; and for this you need a degree of single-mindedness, a willingness to discover what is realistically required, and a determination to carry it out. This is the sense in which you must *want* a PhD. And this 'wanting' is important in that it has to work very hard for you. For example, it has to carry you through occasions when what you are doing may seem very pointless or fruitless, or when you ask yourself the question 'Why have I got myself into this?' or 'Why am I inflicting this on my family?' You cannot expect with an activity as demanding as doing a PhD that the intrinsic satisfaction (such as the interest of doing the research, the enjoyment of discussing your subject with other like-minded researchers) will be sufficient on its own to carry you through. You must always have a clear eye on the extrinsic satisfactions (your commitment to the whole exercise of doing a PhD, its necessary place in your career progression, and so on); you must *want* to do it.

There are, unfortunately, many who turn up as beginning PhD students who do not want to do a PhD in this sense. Particularly vulnerable are those who are using the PhD process as a vehicle for a career change:

● Iris, a teacher for many years, developed an interest in a particular specialism (multi-ethnic curriculum development) and thought she would like to do research in order to establish herself in this new subject. She found that doing research was taking her farther and farther away from dealing with what she saw as the real issues of pupils in the classroom in favour of a measurement-orientated form of 'science' to which she was unsympathetic. She left.

● Jim was a journalist specializing in industrial issues. He wanted an academic career and started a PhD on a politically topical issue. He continued to write occasional newspaper articles to earn money as a student. After producing a series of articles as his inadequate research proposal, his supervisor told him he had to design a questionnaire. He did so and got a group of managers to complete it, but he never analysed it – he said that he didn't see the point. And, of course, there *was* no point – *for him*. He withdrew.

## Not understanding the nature of a PhD by overestimating what is required

The words used to describe the outcome of a PhD project – 'an original contribution to knowledge' – may sound rather grand, but we must remember that, as we saw in Chapter 3, the work for the degree is essentially a *research training* process and the term 'original contribution' has perforce to be interpreted quite narrowly. It does not mean an enormous breakthrough which has the subject rocking on its foundations, and research students who think that it does (even if only subconsciously or in a half-formed way) will find the process pretty debilitating.

Of course, if you are capable of a major contribution then go ahead and make it (there are still, for example, a few scientists who have an FRS but not a PhD) – but this is a strategy for getting an honorary degree, not for getting a PhD! For those not in that position – i.e., most of us – an original contribution can be rather limited in its scope and indeed should be: apply this theory in a different setting, evaluate the effects of raising the temperature, solve this puzzling oddity or review this little-known historical event.

We find that when we make this point, some social science students who have read Kuhn's (1970) work on 'paradigm shifts' in the history of natural science (science students have normally not heard of him) say rather indignantly: 'Oh, do you mean a PhD has to be just doing normal science?' And indeed we do mean that. Paradigm shifts are major changes in the science's explanatory schemes, which happen only rarely when the in-adequacies of the previous framework have become more and more limiting. Normal science is the ordinary research that goes on between major theoretical changes. It serves to elaborate the general explanatory paradigm used and to tease out difficulties and puzzles that are not yet sufficiently well explained. It is the basic useful activity of scientists and scholars, and PhD students should be pleased to make a contribution to it.

You can leave the paradigm shifts for *after* your PhD. And, empirically, that is indeed what happens. The theory of relativity (a classic example of a paradigm shift in relation to post-Newtonian physics) was not Einstein's PhD thesis (that was a sensible contribution to Brownian motion theory). *Das Kapital* was not Marx's PhD (that was on the theories of a little-known Greek philosopher). Of course, while doing their PhDs Einstein and Marx were undoubtedly preparing themselves for the great questionings that led to the big shifts, but they were also demon-strating their fully professional mastery of the established para-digms.

As we saw in Chapter 3, it is this professionalism that the PhD is about. To think it is more than that can be very debilitating. You can wait for a long time for a new paradigm to strike. Over-estimating is a powerful way of not getting a PhD. Here are two classic cases:

● Bob insisted that it would not be 'real' research if he read up in books and journals what others had done on the problem that he wished to tackle; his thinking would be entirely shaped by what they had done and he would only be able to add something minor. He felt that his only chance of being really innovative was not to read anything further in the field (he had a bachelor's and a relevant master's degree in the subject) but to sit down and design an investigation into the problem he was proposing to research (concerned with adult learning of skills), which he knew well from a practical point of view as an industrial trainer. This took quite a long time, as his knowledge of research methods was not that strong.

When he did present his proposal to Dr Bishop, his super-visor, she was not impressed. As this field was not her own particular speciality, Dr Bishop went to the library and looked up all the current year's issues of the relevant journals. In one of them she found a paper reporting a study on Bob's topic that (not surprisingly, since it was completed and published) was considerably better than Bob's attempt. She used this paper to support her argument that he would have to make a comprehensive search of relevant published material if he were to have a chance of designing an adequate study which would make a contribution. But Bob saw this as a negation of what he wanted to do and withdrew.

- While Phil was carrying out the fieldwork stage of his research into the motivation of managers, he became very involved with his subjects. He felt that it would be a betrayal if they were to get no benefit from his research because it was written up in a dull academic book that no one would read. Most research was like that, Phil maintained, and was therefore neglected by everyone except the next lot of researchers. What was needed was a research report that could really communicate. Why couldn't we have a PhD thesis that would read like a novel so that it would become accessible?

Phil took this idea very seriously. He wrote to a novelist whose works he admired for some suggestions on how to write his thesis. He took an extra year to write up the material, letting no one see anything on the way, on the grounds that you don't show a novel to anyone until it is completed. When he did finally present his complete thesis, his supervisor thought it was inadequate, unrigorous and indulgently subjective. Phil was asked to rewrite it, but he refused and thus did not get a PhD.

We hasten to emphasize that this example is not intended to depreciate writing research results for lay people, a very necessary activity that all researchers should take seriously. It is about overestimating what can be done with a PhD and therefore falling flat on your face. Nor does it mean that in writing for your academic peers you should neglect clear expression and interesting presentation – as we discuss in Chapter 6.

## Not understanding the nature of a PhD by underestimating what is required

Underestimating what is required is, we find, particularly a problem for those researching part-time and continuing in their jobs, and for those coming back to academic life after a long period in the 'real world', as they see it. It is basically the difficulty of understanding what is meant by 'research', since the word is used much more strictly in the academic than in the non-academic sphere. We shall discuss the nature of research activity in detail in Chapter 5, but here we can just note that the lay person's view that 'research is finding out something you don't know' is not adequate: that most of the activities described as 'market research' or 'research for a TV programme' do not fulfil the criteria of research required for a PhD.

PhD research requires a contribution to the analysis and explanation of the topic, not just description. It requires an understanding that it is as important a part of the research process to fashion the questions properly as it is to develop interesting answers. It is an underestimation of what is required to accept a 'lay' formulation of either questions or answers – even if they somehow appear more 'relevant' – and it is a clear way of not getting a PhD. Here are two examples:

- Tom was a management consultant who decided to take a three-year sabbatical in order to do a PhD and thus enhance his marketability. He had noted in his job that the time horizons that managers used when making decisions affected the decisions made, and he decided to do his research on this topic, to explore ways of helping managers make better decisions. He took a typical consultant's approach, going round to a number of managers and talking to them about their decision-making problems. He wrote up some particular cases, some particular problems, and some suggestions for getting better decisions made.

  After some months, a few of his clients with whom he had kept in touch and who knew of his new interest began to ask him for help and advice in improving decision-making in their firms. Tom felt that he helped them and therefore that his work was on the right lines. What he wanted to do was write up his knowledge and experience on managers' time horizons, present this as his PhD thesis, publish it as a book, and henceforth be an authority on this subject, thus obtaining more consulting opportunities.

  It took until the end of his first year to convince Tom that, while his approach was a sensible career strategy in itself and his consulting opportunities would certainly improve if he published a book that was interesting and useful to managers, it was not a strategy for obtaining a PhD. His approach seriously underestimated what was required, and he was not doing research in the terms which are necessary for a PhD.

When Tom accepted this, he decided that in that case a PhD
was not worth doing anyway, and withdrew.

● Chris was a financial manager who thought that a research
degree would be a good insurance should he wish in the
future to become a management lecturer. He wanted to do his
research on the financial control systems of his firm, about
which he naturally knew a very great deal. He thought that it
would be easy to do some research into a topic on which he
was one of *the* experts, but he seriously underestimated the
fact that research means finding good questions as well as
good answers.

Chris was not able to formulate research questions himself;
when his supervisor began suggesting a number of questions
that he might investigate, he would take them up enthusiasti-
cally in discussion and give 'the answer' as he knew it to be.
After treating a series of possible topics in this way, it became
clear that he really did not have any need to do research since
he knew all the answers anyway – at least at a level that satisfied him. After it was borne in on him that research requires
actively challenging old explanations and finding new ones if
necessary, his enthusiasm waned and he dropped out.

## Not having a supervisor who knows what a PhD requires

If it is important for a student not to over- or under-estimate the
nature of a PhD, it is equally important to have a supervisor who
does not do so. We shall be discussing issues of supervision in
detail in Chapters 8 and 9, and so here we will just point out that:
(i) inadequate supervision is a major cause of not getting a PhD;
and (ii) since the penalties to students of not succeeding are
much greater than to their supervisors, in the end it is up to
determined students to get the supervision they need and are
entitled to.

● Sophia came to Britain on a government scholarship from a
country that has little tradition of empirical research in her
field. She was allocated to a supervisor who had good practical experience but who had not in fact done any research
himself. She worked away by herself, with occasional comments from him that he thought a particular section very
interesting. But he had badly underestimated the nature of a
PhD. When she submitted her thesis the external examiner

said that, in his opinion, it was so completely inadequate that there was no point in having the oral examination or in allowing a resubmission. She returned to her country sadder, if not wiser.

- Professor Shepherd is a supervisor very few of whose students finish their PhDs. This is surprising, because he is a well known academic in his field, has a lively intelligence and an outgoing personality – which is why he continues to attract students to supervise. But Professor Shepherd believes in treating research students as adults, as he puts it – forgetting that students are babes, in research terms! He believes that it is the supervisor's job to challenge his students, to shake them up mentally, to bombard them with new ideas. He goes on doing this throughout the duration of the research, even when more convergence, more limitations are required to complete the study. Because of this overestimation, many students find they have taken on too large a project, which they do not see becoming more focused. They get disheartened and drop out.

## Losing contact with your supervisor

As we said above, the penalties of failure are greater for the student than for the supervisor. The relationship is not one of equality, so the student has to work harder to keep in touch with the supervisor than the other way around. As we discussed in Chapter 3, the nature of the PhD process requires continual input from the supervisor if the student is to learn the craft of research and how to apply it to the particular topic under study. The details of managing this interaction fruitfully on both sides are covered in Chapters 8 and 9. Here we will just illustrate the inevitably catastrophic effect which results if contact is lost.

- Tony got bogged down 18 months into his project. After a long session with his supervisor he decided that he wanted to change direction. His supervisor said that it was impossible to do so at this stage and he should carry on – even though it was now clear that more work would be required than originally envisaged, with a weaker outcome anyway. Tony did not agree and tried to persuade his supervisor to allow greater modifications. His supervisor explained that this was not sensible within the available timescale, and pressed him to carry on with the original design. They saw each other less and less because Tony felt that they were talking at cross-purposes. After four months they ceased to have any meetings; after six months Tony was observed rushing into a lecture room to avoid his supervisor whom he saw coming towards him along the corridor. He never submitted his thesis.

- David's supervisor, Professor Dickinson, was one of the leading academics in Britain in her field. She died tragically when David was at the end of his second year. His supervision was taken over by an experienced researcher whose range of concerns was different and who had only a general interest in David's topic.

David did not think it necessary to tell his new supervisor in any detail what he was doing, having it clear in his mind that Professor Dickinson would have given her approval. He thus worked without supervision for a further 18 months. The result was that when he came to submit his thesis he had, in effect, *two* external examiners, since his supervisor/internal examiner knew as little about the work as the external examiner. Both felt that he had suffered from lack of supervision, which in the circumstances should be taken into account, but that they could award him only an MPhil, not a PhD. He appealed, but in due course the university confirmed the decision.

David's enforced change of supervisor was due to a particularly tragic event. Supervisors leave for happier reasons too, and often it is necessary to be handed on to another supervisor. In these circumstances it is particularly incumbent on the student to make good contact with the new supervisor, whose knowledge and skills are a crucial input to getting a PhD.

### Not having a thesis

Words develop in meaning, and the word 'thesis' is nowadays commonly used to refer to the project report of the research undertaken for the PhD. Thus the regulations of your university or the CNAA may say that your thesis may be not more than a certain number of words in length, that it must be presented in black/blue/red binding, and so on. (Incidentally, these regulations differ for different institutions and they also change over time, so it is important for you to check those which apply to you, as discussed in Chapter 10.)

But there is an earlier use of the word 'thesis' that is very important to the task of obtaining a PhD. A thesis in this sense is something that you wish to argue, a *position* that you wish to maintain (the word 'thesis' derives from the Greek for 'place'). For example, the Reformation began when Martin Luther nailed a list of 95 theses to the door of Wittenberg Church – statements of his beliefs, which he wished to maintain against the Roman church of that time. C. P. Snow propounded the thesis that British intellectuals inhabit two separate cultures – literary and scientific – which hardly overlap. It is *our* thesis that it is crucial for students wanting to obtain a PhD that they understand fully the objectives of the exercise and the nature of the processes involved, which is why we have written this book.

Your PhD must have a thesis in this sense. It must argue a position. At the minimum this means that the study must have a 'story line', a coherent thrust which pushes along an argument, an explanation, a systematic set of inferences derived from new data or new ways of viewing current data. It is not enough for your thesis report to be 'a short trot with a cultured mind', in Patrick Campbell's memorable phrase.

It may be that the thesis you are arguing has been decomposed into a number of 'hypo-theses' (usually pronounced hy*poth*eses) each of which will be tested for its adequacy. In this case you must relate them to each other to maintain the general thrust of your argument. If you are not working in the hypothesis-testing mode you must still ensure that your discussions add up to a coherent argument. This is how the adequacy of your contribution is judged.

As with all the other ways of not getting a PhD, this is easier to say than to do, particularly if you do not have good guidance in the early stages of your research, when the temptation to spread yourself too widely and too thinly is greatest.

- Harry started out to study factors affecting industrial marketing strategies. This is a large field and he was able to tackle the issues only rather superficially. Some of the chapters in his thesis report made some good points, others were rather poor, but none of the aspects was at all related to the others in a cumulative way. The examiners said that his thesis 'did not add up to anything' and rejected it.
- Graham was the administrator of a voluntary organization. He registered for a PhD because he felt that not enough was known about how to manage such organizations; more

research was needed to make administrators in this field more professional. He spent his first year reading a great deal about administration and thinking how the ideas could be applied to help administrators in voluntary organizations. When he was asked how his research could help them, he said that he wanted to write a textbook describing good administrative practices. There then followed a long period of trying to get through to him that without a thesis his work would not earn a PhD, though it might well be a useful thing to do in itself. In the end he reluctantly accepted this.

We must emphasize that it is not the notion of a textbook *per se* that makes it inadequate for a PhD but the lack of a thesis. A textbook which incorporated a well argued, justified thesis – for example, that accepted views are inadequate when the data are critically re-examined, or that the field can be reinterpreted fruitfully in the light of a new theory – would be very acceptable.

## Taking a new job before finishing

Doing a PhD is an intellectually demanding enterprise, and this is true at all stages of the work. It is especially true of the final stage of writing up. Most students radically underestimate the amount of time and effort that this stage will require. They somehow think that having surveyed the field, designed the study, collected and analysed the data, it is downhill from then on to the presentation of the thesis. It is not so. Writing up demands the most concentrated effort of the whole process.

There are a number of reasons for this. The first is emotional: it is difficult to avoid feeling that this is a chore, after the 'real' work has been done. There are always ambivalent feelings about the study itself and a barely suppressed desire to run away from it all, now that the data are actually there for others to see. The second reason is intellectual: unless you are extremely lucky and everything turns out exactly as planned, there will at this stage be quite a lot of adjustment to be done in your argument, in your interpretation, in your presentation, to put the best face on the material you have available. This is an extremely demanding test of professional competence, and it is in fact at *this* stage that you have really to demonstrate that you are worth a PhD.

There is a third reason concerned with limitations in writing skill and experience. Few students have written anything as long as a PhD thesis before, and to complete it requires a considerable effort.

For all these reasons, writing up is not the time to take a new job. Apart from the physical dislocation, which makes intellectual work difficult and therefore easily postponed, a new job is likely to require you to concentrate your attention on a new range of issues, which, particularly if they are academic ones, will inevitably get in the way of writing up, through intellectual fatigue.

The only job it is possible to do, perhaps one which you are doing already or have done before, is one which allows you to operate in 'intellectual overdrive'. Taking a *new* job before finishing is a way of not getting a PhD. At the very least it will put off completion for several years (in our experience six to eight years and more), until the intellectual learning curve of the new job allows it – or else you join the ranks of those whom the Americans call the 'ABDs': the 'all-but-dissertation' brigade.

## Action summary

1 Be aware of the seven ways of not getting a PhD:
   – not wanting a PhD;
   – overestimating what is required;
   – underestimating what is required;
   – having a supervisor who does not know what is required;
   – losing contact with your supervisor;
   – not having a 'thesis' (i.e., position, argument) to maintain;
   – taking a *new* job before completing.
2 Work to understand the implications of these traps fully in your own situation and determine not to succumb to them.
3 Re-establish your determination regularly when blandishments to stray from your programme of work recur.

# 5
# How to do research

What is research? This is not as simple a question as it seems. In this chapter we are going to explore some answers to it and examine their relevance to the nature of a PhD.

## Characteristics of research

Let us start with a basic lay view: 'Research is finding out something you don't know.' This answer is both too wide and too narrow. It is too wide because it includes many activities, such as finding out the time of the next train to London, or taking the temperature of the water in the swimming pool, which we would not characterize as research. Take a moment to consider why we would not do so. And if we were measuring instead the pH value of the water – its acidity – would that be research?

As well as being too wide, that definition is also too narrow, because a lot of research is concerned not with 'finding out something you don't know' but with 'finding that you don't know something'. This sort of research aims to reorient our thinking, to make us question what we think we do know, and to focus on new aspects of our complex reality.

In exploring the nature of research, it is useful to distinguish it from another activity: intelligence-gathering.

## Intelligence-gathering – the 'what' questions

There are a lot of things that we don't know and that we could find out. What are the age, sex and subject distributions of doctoral students in British higher education? What are the radiation levels in different parts of the country? What percentage of the GNP is spent on scientific research? These 'what' questions are very important. They require careful definition of terms, unbiased collection of information, meticulous statistical treatment and careful summarizing to get a balanced description of the situation that gives 'a true and fair picture' – to use a phrase from the accounting profession. Inevitably some arbitary decisions will have to be made. Conventions are developed which can help to improve comparability – in the measurement of high temperatures, the definition of the money supply, the genetic classification into male and female sexes, etc. – but professionals can and do differ on what they regard as fair, and informed judgement is called for. For example, it is a matter of considerable controversy at present as to what would be a true and fair way to define, and therefore count and categorize, the number of unemployed, the level of radiation tolerable in the atmosphere, and so on.

Since this work is descriptive, answering the 'what' questions, it can be considered as 'intelligence-gathering' – using the term in the military sense. Intelligence-gathering is an important activity and intelligence is a valued commodity. A profit-and-loss account of a business, a map giving radiation levels in different parts of the country, a compilation of the evaluations by doctoral students of the quality of supervision they receive, are all examples of intelligence with important uses.

We may use the profit-and-loss account as part of a financial control system, the radiation-level map to develop nuclear siting policies, the doctoral students' evaluations to make decisions on selection and training of supervisors, etc. Control mechanisms, policy formulation and decision-making are the typical uses of intelligence. These are all absolutely vital activities – but they are not research.

## Research – the 'why' questions

Research goes beyond description and requires analysis. It looks for explanations, relationships, comparisons, predictions, generalizations and theories. These are the 'why' questions. Why are there so many fewer women doctoral students in physics than in biology? Why are the radiation levels different in different areas? Why is the GNP in Britain increasing more slowly than in other countries?

All these questions require good intelligence-gathering, just as decision-making and policy formulation do. But the information is used for the purpose of developing understanding – by comparison, by relating to other factors, by theorizing and testing the theories. All research questions have comparisons in them, as the words 'fewer', 'different' and 'more slowly' in the examples above illustrate. All research questions also involve generalization. To be useful, explanations should be applicable in all appropriate situations.

## Characteristics of good research

There are three distinct but interrelated characteristics of good research which distinguish this activity from others such as intelligence-gathering, decision-making and so on.

### (i) Research is based on an open system of thought

For you as a researcher, the world is in principle your oyster. You are entitled to think anything. There are no hidden agendas, no closed systems; in American terms, 'everything is up for grabs'. This continual testing, review and criticism *for its own sake* by researchers of each other's work is an important way in which thinking develops. Conventional wisdom and accepted doctrine are not spared this examination because they may turn out to be inadequate. Of course they may not turn out to be inadequate – they may stand up to examination. This is why non-researchers often regard research results as being demonstrations of the obvious or trivial elaborations of established knowledge. But this examination has to be done continually because this is how we probe for what is not obvious and discover elaborations that are not trivial. The key to the approach is to keep firmly in mind that the classic position of a researcher is not that of one who knows the right answers but of one who is struggling to find out what the right questions might be!

### (ii) Researchers examine data critically

This characteristic of research is clearly part of the first one. We list it separately because it is probably the most important single element in distinguishing a research approach from others and researchers from practitioners and lay people. Researchers examine data and the sources of data critically, so that the basic research approach to provocative statements ('women make less effective managers than men', 'soft drugs are less harmful to health than alcohol') is not to agree or disagree but to ask: 'What is your evidence?'

Researchers are continually having to ask: 'Have you got the facts right? Can we get better data? Can the results be interpreted differently?' Non-researchers often feel that they don't have the time for this and are thus impatient with research. Politicians and managers, for example, often need to make decisions under constraints of public pressure or time. Their need to act is more important than their need to understand. Researchers' priorities are, of course, different. They have to go to great trouble to get systematic, valid and reliable data because their aim is to understand and interpret.

### (iii) Researchers generalize and specify the limits on their generalizations

It is the aim of research to obtain valid generalizations because this is the most efficient way of applying understanding in a wide variety of appropriate situations – but there are difficulties here. It was not a researcher but a novelist, Alexandre Dumas, who said: 'All generalizations are dangerous – including this one!' Indeed, research may be said to proceed by insightful but dangerous generalizations, which is why the limits of the generalization – where it applies and where it does not apply – must be continually tested.

The way generalizations can best be established is through the development of explanatory theory, and it is indeed the application of theory that turns intelligence-gathering into research. So to return to the question asked at the beginning of this chapter: would measuring the pH value of the water in a swimming pool be research? The answer would depend upon what we were going to do with the result – not on how complicated or how 'scientific' the measurement was. If the result were used to develop and test a theory of the factors that determine the acidity of water, it would be research; if it were used to make a decision on whether the pool was safe, then it would be intelligence-gathering.

## Basic types of research

Research has traditionally been classified into two types: pure and applied. But we find that this distinction – implying as it does that pure research supplies the theories and applied research uses and tests them out in the real world – is too rigid to characterize what happens in most academic disciplines, where, for example, 'real-world' research generates its own theories and does not just apply 'pure' theories. We shall consider a threefold classification of research: exploratory, testing-out and problem-solving.

### (i) Exploratory research

This is the type of research that is involved in tackling a new problem, issue, topic about which little is known, so the research idea cannot at the beginning be formulated very well. The problem may come from any part of the discipline; it may be a theoretical research puzzle or have an empirical basis. The research work will need to examine what theories and concepts are appropriate, developing new ones if necessary, and whether existing methodologies can be used. It obviously involves pushing out the frontiers of knowledge in the hope that something useful will be discovered.

### (ii) Testing-out research

In this type of research we are trying to find the limits of previously proposed generalizations. As we have discussed above, this is a basic research activity. Does the theory apply at high temperatures? In new-technology industries? With working-class parents? Before universal franchise was introduced? The amount of testing out to be done is endless and continuous, because in this way we are able to improve (by specifying, modifying, clarifying) the important, but dangerous, generalizations by which our discipline develops.

### (iii) Problem-solving research

In this type of research, we start from a particular problem 'in the real world', and bring together all the intellectual resources that can be brought to bear on its solution. The problem has to be defined and the method of solution has to be discovered. The person working in this way may have to create and identify original problem solutions every step of the way. This will usually involve a variety of theories and methods, often ranging across more than one discipline since real-world problems are likely to be 'messy' and not soluble within the narrow confines of an academic discipline.

## Which type of research for the PhD?

Since we spent so much time in Chapter 4 discussing how *not* to get a PhD, let us now look on the more positive side and ask how to *get* a doctorate. Consider for a moment the three types of research that we have just reviewed. Which type is likely to offer the best chance of completing the degree successfully? Remember that we have already noted that the PhD is primarily a research *training* exercise to get you from being a mere beginner in research to the level of a full professional. All research involves working within particular constraints, but those of a PhD are very stringent. They include clear limitations on finance, physical resources, administrative backup and, above all, time. So which of the three types of research would you choose as the best route at this stage of your career? Take a few moments to consider your decision and the reasons for it.

We hope that you will understand why it seems very obvious to us that the appropriate route is that of testing-out research. With this approach you will be working within an established framework and thus learning the craft of doing research in an environment that gives you some degree of protection by the established nature of much of the ideas, arguments, measuring equipment, etc. A degree of protection in the environment is the best situation for efficient learning: being thrown in at the deep end is all very heroic but it does tend to induce a phenomenon known as drowning!

Of course, you will have to make your original contribution – merely replicating what others have done is not adequate. So, for example, you will have to use a methodology on a new topic where it has not been applied before and therefore make manifest its strengths in giving new knowledge and theoretical insights. Or you will have to apply two competing theories to a new situation to see which is more powerful, or design a crucial experiment to produce evidence to choose between them. As a result you may produce your own innovative variant of the methodology or theory. So there will always be an appropriate element of exploratory work and you may well solve some useful *discipline-based* problems on the way. Testing out is the basic ongoing professional task of academic research, and doctoral work done well in this framework is much more likely to be *useful* and thus publishable and quotable.

On the other hand, the idea, of tackling an exploratory topic which has little by way of conceptual frameworks, or of solving a real-world problem seems very attractive. (This is particularly so for social scientists, who often have the impression, wrongly, that their undergraduate degree studies have given them all they need to know about the discipline and they can therefore tackle any topic in it.)

There is no denying the attraction of tackling such topics, but you should be aware that the risks of failure are much greater. If you have a lot of confidence, stemming, say, from a great deal of practical experience *and* very strong support from your supervisor (who will inevitably be called upon to make a larger input) you might consider work in the exploratory or problem-solving approaches. But these are undoubtedly less structured and therefore professionally more advanced activities, and most students should be considering whether they can run before they can walk.

It is also fair to point out that even if you obtain a PhD for work that is completely exploratory or problem-solving, which is less likely anyway, there will almost inevitably be a considerable element of giving credit for a 'brave try' (examiners being kind people who look for ways of passing students). So in these circumstances it is *less* likely that your work will make sufficient impact to be publishable and quotable than if you do well in the testing-out approach. It will then serve you less well as a base on which to build a research career. It is a wise student who decides to postpone the pleasures of attempting to be totally original until after the PhD has been obtained.

## The craft of doing research

Doing research is a craft skill, which is why the basic educational process that takes place is that of learning by doing. After you have decided on your research approach and the particular field in which you are going to learn your craft, you should be systematically considering how you are going to get the training that you require in each of the craft elements.

These are many and varied, and depend on your particular discipline. So your first task is to watch established good researchers in your discipline and note down, as systematically as you can, what practices, skills and techniques they are using. Hopefully your supervisor will be one of these researchers, but you must examine and learn from others too.

Your second task is to practise these skills as much as you can, *getting feedback on how well you are doing*. Adults learn best in situations where they can practise and receive feedback, in a controlled, non-threatening environment. So a good principle to aim for is: *no procedure, technique, skill, etc., which is relevant to your thesis project should be exercised by you there for the first time*. You should always have practised it beforehand on a non-thesis exercise, which is therefore going to be less stressful and will allow for greater learning. Your trial exercises will allow you to learn about your ability to carry out the range of professional skills that you need to develop. You will gain feedback, not only from your supervisor but also other professionals (e.g. computer people) and from your own evaluation of what you have done.

This may seem an eminently sensible principle, and you may wonder why we are labouring it. After all it is obvious that skills need to be practised if they are to be performed well. An art student doesn't expect the first oil painting she ever attempted to be exhibited at the Royal Academy, a poet doesn't expect his first poem to be publishable. They are likely to be apprentice pieces, learning experiences.

In fact, as regards PhD skills this issue is often not thought through well enough. If the thesis report, which may be 50–60,000 words long, is the first thing that the student has written longer than the answer to an examination question, a term essay or a lab report, then it is not surprising that it is a daunting task, poorly done. The skill practice has just not taken place. Analysing your data from the key experiment or survey you have just carried out is precisely *not* the time to discover for the first time the joys of getting your data into, and the results out of, a computer. You should have practised that craft skill beforehand. Again, it does not seem sensible to base your PhD thesis study on the first faltering questionnaire that you have ever tried to devise – but all too often people do, and later pay the price for their inevitably less than skilled performance in questionnaire design.

There are many more examples which we could discuss of the skills which a doctoral student needs to set about acquiring. They range from the seemingly mundane but absolutely crucial ones of maintaining your lab apparatus and conducting a computer-based literature search to the more conceptual ones of being able to evaluate quickly the relevance and value of published work. You will need to have found out what craft skills are relevant to your needs and to have practised them, so that in your thesis project you can apply them with some confidence.

## Self-help and peer support groups

Working towards the PhD is usually experienced as an isolating and lonely time. This need not be the case. If you can arrange to meet regularly with others in your situation, you will find that you can help yourself and them in several ways.

The first, and most obvious, is that you are no longer in solitary confinement, with nobody interested in your work, aware of what you are doing, or concerned about how you are feeling with regard to the postgraduate degree. You will discover, when you feel depressed and discouraged and are thinking seriously about 'dropping out', that this is part of the general malaise of post-graduate life and not peculiar to you and your inadequacies. Once you become aware that such feelings are experienced by the majority of research students from time to time, you will be able to put them into perspective as part of the process that has to be got through, instead of seeing them as proof of your own incompetence.

Further, once you are able to share these feelings and to talk about them and their effect on your work, you will all start to feel better. As one of the group confronts the problems, the others will be able to help, and when it comes to their turn they will remember how it was and know that it is possible to get through it. This may sound a little like Alcoholics Anonymous and that is precisely what it is, but the difference is that you are trying to *continue* doing research and writing it up, rather than trying to give up doing something.

A more pragmatic function for your group or peer (just one other postgraduate at your stage of the PhD is sufficient) is to help in keeping you to deadlines. Each of you states what work you want to do and sets a time limit for its completion. This commitment serves as a motivator. When that date arrives you meet, as already arranged, and talk about your progress. If you have done what you intended, then set another time limit for the next piece of work. If you have not done what you intended, discuss with the other(s) why this is so, what the problems were and how you feel about not having got to where you were aiming. Sometimes it is acceptable not to have continued because of things that have been discovered *en route* or because of overambitious planning. As long as these reasons are not just rationalizations, then there is nothing to be concerned about. But if, on the other hand, you are dejected because of your failure to produce on time, then you need to talk about what happened in some detail. Once things have been clarified and you and your peer group are satisfied that the way is now clear to proceed you can set new deadlines for the same, or a somewhat modified, piece of work.

Another positive function for this group of two or more people is to provide feedback on written work. It is not even necessary for you to be working in the same discipline. As long as your areas of research are reasonably comprehensible to each other, which is usually the case within a faculty, then there is no need for any real knowledge of the topic. For example, Evelyn, a social psychologist, and Joyce, a geographer, helped each other with drafts of their thesis chapters even though neither knew anything about the other's discipline. They were both social scientists, understood research methodology and statistics appropriate to the social sciences, and were able to read and understand English. This was sufficient for them to be of great help to each other until quite an advanced stage of thesis writing. They questioned that which they did not understand, which helped the writer to clarify her thinking and explain it more simply. They criticized complicated sentence structure and confusion in the structural development of a line of thought. They queried quantum leaps from the results of the research to interpretations based on the results, and generally learned from each other how to improve their own work, while also becoming interested in the other's research for its own sake. They are both convinced that they would never have completed their theses and gained their PhDs within the time they set themselves if they had not formed this self-help group of two. They are still firm friends several years later, and each proudly has a copy of the other's thesis.

**Action summary**

1 Consider very carefully the advantage of doing 'testing-out' research for your PhD.
2 From observation and discussion with your supervisor and other academics, construct a list of the craft practices that characterize a good professional researcher in your discipline.

3 Aim to ensure that no procedure, technique, skill, etc., that is
  relevant to your project will be exercised by you there for the
  first time.
4 Establish a peer support group with at least one other PhD
  student in order to give mutual criticism and encouragement
  and to act as monitor on time deadlines.

# 6
# The form of a PhD thesis

Three of the key ways of not getting a PhD that we discussed in Chapter 4 involved either the student or the supervisor (or both) not understanding the nature of a PhD degree. This demonstration that you are a full professional requires the exercise of the craft of doing research, as discussed in Chapter 5, in such a way as to satisfy the examiners (i.e., your senior professional peers) that you are in full command of your academic field.

This you do by 'making a contribution to knowledge'. This sounds both very impressive and extremely vague, and is therefore quite worrying to students. In this chapter we shall examine what form of a PhD thesis will satisfy these requirements.

## Understanding the PhD form

Once again we must start by explaining that, as with the nature of a PhD, it is not possible to spell out administratively or bureaucratically what is required – that is not the nature of the process. The university regulations for a doctorate, for example, have to apply in all subject fields from Arabic to zoology. So they are inevitably formal and are not able to catch the particular requirements in *your* field at *this* time. Indeed the aim of the training process is precisely to put you in a position where you can evaluate what is required, in addition to being capable of carrying it out.

There is, however, a certain *form* to doctoral theses – clearly at a high level of abstraction, since it has to be independent of the content and apply to all fields of knowledge. We may think of the analogy of the sonata form in music. This is a structure of musical writing, but it tells you nothing about the content. Haydn wrote in sonata form (he more or less invented it) but so did the Beatles. The range of content covered is therefore enormous *but* the sonata form does not cover all music. Neither Debussy nor Britten used this form. In jazz Scott Joplin used sonata form but Bix Beiderbecke did not. The same is the case with the PhD. It has a particular form and since not all research conforms to it, you have to be aware of what the elements of its form are.

There are four elements to PhD form that we have to consider: background theory; focal theory; data theory; and contribution.

## Background theory

This is the field of study within which you are working and which you must know well – i.e., to full professional standard. So you must be aware of the present state of the art: what developments, controversies, breakthroughs are currently exciting or enraging the leading practitioners and thus pushing forward thinking in the subject.

The standard way of demonstrating this is through a literature review. Remember that you are not doing a literature review for its own sake; you are doing it in order to demonstrate that you have a fully professional grasp of the background theory to your subject. 'Professional' means, as we saw in Chapter 3, that you have something to say about your field that your fellow professionals would want to listen to. So organizing the material in an interesting and useful way, evaluating the contributions of others (and justifying the criticisms, of course), identifying trends in research activity, defining areas of theoretical and empirical weakness, are all key activities by which you would demonstrate that you had a professional command of the background theory.

It is important to emphasize that a mere encyclopaedic listing in which all the titles were presented with only a description of each work and no reasoned organization and evaluation would not be adequate. It would not demonstrate the professional judgement that is required of a PhD. It would be the equivalent of your taking a driving test and driving at no more than 20 mph throughout. You would fail because you had not demonstrated sufficient confidence and competence to be in charge of a vehicle. As a PhD, you must similarly be confidently and competently in charge of your understanding of background theory, and you have to demonstrate this through the literature review.

For this part of your task you can, in many disciplines, get a good idea of the style and standard of the approach that is required by reading the literature surveys that comprise the 'annual reviews' in the subject. The *Annual Reviews* of biochemistry, economics, etc., contain such reviews of the background theory of parts of the discipline, contributed by leading scholars in the field. You can discover therefore how they evaluate, shape and focus their topics in ways which encourage further fruitful research. It is that degree of command to which you should aspire.

### Focal theory

The second element in the form of the PhD is the 'focal theory'. It is here that you spell out in great detail precisely what you are researching and why. You establish the nature of your problem and set about analysing it. The generation of hypotheses, if appropriate, the examination of others' arguments, the use of your own data and analysis to push forward the academic discussion are the key tasks here.

It is in the carrying out of your work on the focal theory that, as we saw in Chapter 4, it is vital to have a thesis in the narrow sense. This gives a clear 'story line' and enables you to relate what you are doing to the focal theory in an organized way. Your thesis and the need to support it with your data and arguments perform important work for you as the criteria for what it is relevant to include in your study. You should therefore be very careful to ensure that the argument is not blurred with extraneous or makeweight material that is not contributing to the maintenance of your thesis position. The thesis of the focal theory should always be in focus!

### Data theory

The third element of the PhD form is the data theory. In the most general terms this gives the justification for the relevance and validity of the material that you are going to use to support your thesis. A key question in the evaluation of your work must be: why should we (your fellow academics in the field) have to listen to you? You must clearly have a convincing answer.

Just what the content of your data theory is will vary enormously from discipline to discipline, but the form will always be concerned with the appropriateness and reliability of your data sources. In the sciences it will entail the demonstration that your apparatus is sensitive enough to detect the effect and is reliably calibrated. In historical studies you will need to show that your documents are adequate and properly interpreted. In the social sciences you might need to engage in an epistemological discussion about which interpretative framework (e.g., positivist, Marxist) it is appropriate for you to use to maintain your position.

Identifying just what an adequate discussion of the data theory for your particular thesis involves is one of the professional tasks that you have to undertake. You do this in discussion with your supervisor, by reviewing the latest papers in your field and by examining successful PhD submissions.

## Contribution

The spelling out of your contribution is the final element in the PhD form. It is concerned with your evaluation of the importance of your thesis to the development of the discipline. It is here that you underline the significance of your analysis, point out the limitations in your material, suggest what new work is now appropriate, and so on. In the most general terms it is a discussion as to why and in what way the background theory and the focal theory that you started with are now different as a result of your research work. Thus your successors (who include, of course, yourself) now face a different situation when determining what their research work should be since they now have to take account of your work.

It might seem strange that you are asked to evaluate your own work, pointing out its limitations, putting it into perspective, and so on. Aren't you likely to think your study is 'the best thing since sliced bread', or at least take a very biased view of it? Well, clearly not, and this is another demonstration of the point that we made in Chapter 3 on the meaning of a doctorate. You are not doing some research for its own sake; you are doing it in order to demonstrate that you are a full professional, with a good grasp of what is happening in your field and capable of evaluating the impact of new contributions to it – your own as well as others'. That is what you get the doctorate for.

In practical terms, this component of the thesis is usually the last chapter or so, and it is very important not to underestimate this task. We have already pointed out in Chapter 4 that it takes much longer than you think to write. Indeed, in our experience its inadequacy is the most common single reason for requiring students to resubmit their theses after first presentation.

There is one particular trap to avoid. If you entitle your last chapter 'Summary and conclusions', and you have no very clear idea of what 'conclusions' would mean, then you will inevitably spend most of your time on the summary. You will know the details of your work very well by this time, and the 'summary' could easily stretch into large amounts of repetition. Then, when you have written most of a chapter, just a short ending does not seem so bad. One of us (DSP) has examined theses where, after an overlong summary, only the final page attempted a conclusion – in one case only in the final paragraph was this ventured. Of course this is inadequate, and such submissions are referred back for the necessary further work to be done.

It is important then:

● to be clear that the summary and the conclusions are quite separate tasks. To underline this, we recommend putting them in separate chapters, but in any case *more* effort needs to go into the conclusions than the summary.
● to have a concept of what purpose the conclusion performs: namely, to demonstrate how the background theory and the focal theory are now different as a result of the study.

### Detailed structure and choice of chapter headings

You may hear people telling you about the 'ideal' length of a thesis. Pay no attention. A thesis should be no longer than it needs to be in order to report what you have done, why you did it and what you have concluded from the results of your work. Don't be impressed by theses that run to two volumes: it is often (correctly) said that a lot is written in order to obscure the fact that little has been achieved. In fact you might adopt the maxim that if you can say it briefly you should do so; but not if this means using lots of long words and complex sentence structures.

A thesis should contain a review of relevant literature, a description of what has been done, what came out of this, a discussion of these results and finally some conclusions that can be drawn and suggestions for future work. Stated baldly, these sections are:

Introduction (including Aims)
Literature survey
Method
Results
Discussion
Conclusions

These general sections can be further subdivided into relevant chapters, depending on your discipline and topic. In addition to the main sections your thesis will require, at the beginning, an abstract that summarizes the work in order to make the job of the examiners easier. There should also be a clear statement of the problem under exploration. Once they know what to expect, the examiners have a frame of reference for reading the thesis. At the end you should have a detailed list of references and any appendices such as graphs, tables, data collection sheets, etc., that do not fit easily into the body of the thesis.

Your university or polytechnic will have detailed information on how they expect the finished article to look, including precise width of margins and wording of the title page. There will also be rules concerning the binding of the thesis and number of copies to be produced. Be sure that you are in possession of all this information so that you do not have a last-minute panic because you failed to adhere to some minor but crucial instruction.

Once you have all these formalities under your control you can begin to have fun with the thesis. Thinking of pertinent but snappy titles for your chapters and subsections is a pleasant diversion from churning out thousands of words which conform to the expectations of supervisors and examiners. Even the title of the thesis itself can be a source of entertainment for a while. Don't go for the dry-as-dust and long-winded descriptive title. Yes, of course the title must bear a relationship to the contents, but that's no reason for it to make what is inside the thesis sound boring. Try to whet the appetite of the reader, arouse the curiosity of the examiner.

One supervisor repeatedly told his students that he expected to be supplied with a thesis that would make bedtime reading, challenging his usual book. He expected to be so engrossed in it that he would be unable to put it down and would read it right through until 2 a.m. or later in order not to spoil the flow. This might sound like an impossible task, but that is no reason not to aim for it. What it means is that you have to use everyday English instead of jargon wherever possible, without losing the precision of definition that is essential. You should also keep to sentences that do not include complicated constructions, such as ever-increasing numbers of embedded clauses. Aim to impress with clarity as well as original and sound research. Remember that even well established experts are human beings, and nobody enjoys turgid prose.

### Writing the thesis

The PhD thesis is the final product. You will be assessed on it as the result of your several years of research work. Yet writing the thesis is far more than merely reporting the outcome of your research. At this important stage students experience a great deal of difficulty and discomfort.

Wason (1974) has described the procrastination and incoherence into which many doctoral candidates fall when attempting to present results in written form. Baddeley (1979) has pointed out the difficulties experienced by most supervisors in the training of students' writing skills and in providing adequate supervision of the writing process. Thus until supervisors have training in this regard you cannot realistically expect very much assistance here. In contrast, Murray (1978) has suggested a technique to improve writing skills. His idea is that students, when writing successive drafts of a report or a chapter, keep them separate; later they should examine the set to see whether succeeding drafts define and refine meaning more effectively than did the earlier ones.

In fact *re*writing is a very important factor in the writing process, and authors often read and rewrite to discover what it is that they have to say. But not everybody goes about writing in the same way. In a study of writing among 170 academic staff members, Lowenthal and Wason (1977) identified two distinct types of writers:

– 'serialists', who see writing as a sequential process in which the words are corrected as they are written and who plan their writing in detail before beginning to write;
– 'holists', who can only think as they write and compose a succession of complete drafts.

They discovered, too, that some of these academics achieved great satisfaction from the act of writing while others described it as an extremely painful experience. So you can see that it is not only postgraduates who suffer the pains and problems of trying to write.

It may be that the difficulty in writing experienced by so many people is due to a strong link between written language and thought. Written language has been referred to as 'the means of discovery of new knowledge' (Olson 1975). If it is the case that writing leads to discovery and not, as is generally supposed, that discoveries merely need to be put into writing, this may in part account for the experience of writing the thesis as the most difficult part of the work. Writing makes people think about their work in a different way.

It is necessary to formulate clearly in writing ideas which you will have got to know very well indeed but which will be new to the reader. You are aiming to impart information and knowledge that you already have to others who do not yet have it, and this means that assumptions have to be made explicit and ideas expressed clearly. The thinking that links one idea with others or that emerges from a particular assumption has to be unambiguously translated into the written language.

Remarks such as 'good writing can't cure bad thought' and 'I can't clearly express in words what I have in my head' are typical of the comments made by thesis-writers and academic staff members alike. Several eminent psychologists interviewed by Cohen (1977) said that the only time they think is when they write and Murray (1978) reports that this is also true of poets and authors. He suggests it may be true of all writing.

One of us found, during a three-year study into learning to do research (Phillips 1984), that postgraduate students in science disciplines discussed the two parts of their work as follows:

> If it's time-consuming and mindless, like just repeating experiments, I like it, but if it's difficult too, like writing an introduction and conclusion, then I don't like it.

> I'd rather potter about in the laboratory during working hours – it's less taxing mentally.

> I prefer to be working with my hands than writing, I don't like a lot of this book work.

This preference shown by scientists for experimental work in the laboratory, including keeping lab books up to date, meant that writing papers or thesis chapters was assigned to evenings, weekends and holidays. It was not perceived as 'real work', and as it was thought to be of only secondary importance it was never undertaken at the time intended. One student said 'I'm doing bits and pieces of writing-up whenever I get a minute' but abandoned every piece of written work commenced during the three-year period.

In fact most research students do tend to postpone writing until their final year, but we advise very strongly indeed against adopting this course of action. Some of the statements made by arts students also demonstrate how *they* feel about writing:

> I hate writing and I'm lousy at it. The thought will come when I put it all together; at present it's still a mechanical process. Once started I know I need to write without a break, it's essential to keep going once started.

> Obviously you don't formulate what you're going to say *completely* until you come to write it down . . . it was only when I was writing it that I realized that in one section my interpretation was completely wrong. The point I was trying to make just wouldn't embody itself verbally, so I thought it out again and rewrote the whole section.

Some of these comments from postgraduates are reminiscent of those made by the academics in the Lowenthal and Wason sample in which the two types of writers were identified. From the student sample we also have the serialist approach:

> It's stylistic, the phrasing of the work and the way it flows, that I'm having difficulty with at the moment. When I do write sentences I feel good about my style. I don't feel like an inadequate writer, but writing sentences is very slow.

The emphasis here on the writing of sentences is very different from the way in which a holistic writer talks about his work:

> I write a complete first draft in longhand. As I go along I tend to revise a bit, but when I've finished I revise a great deal and it tends to look like World War 3 on paper. If I'm really interested in it I'll start at 8.30 a.m. or 9.30 a.m. and go on until late at night. Once I start I want to see it finished, the shorter the time between conception and finished article the better.

The fact that people approach writing in different ways is an important observation because people usually assume that everybody writes in the same way. In fact at school we are all instructed to make a plan and then write the essay. But we are not all 'planners' – some of us are 'get-it-all-out'-ers. It is not at all easy *both* (i) to say what you want to say *and* (ii) to say it in the best possible way *at the same time*. It is sensible, therefore, to do it in stages.

First have to hand those three indispensable props to good writing: a recent edition of a good dictionary, Roget's *Thesaurus* and Gower's *Plain Words*. We recommend that you approach every piece of writing in the following way:

- *generate* the main points (in any order if you're a holist, and sequentially if you're a serialist), putting down everything that comes into your mind;
- *organize* them into an acceptable structure; and only then attempt to
- *construct* the points into grammatical paragraphs made up of well balanced sentences.

This, of course, makes it sound easier than it is, but if you are able to read what you have written as though it were the work of someone else, you will find it less difficult to be critical of your own imprecise phrases and sloppy style. The way to achieve this 'distance' between yourself and your work is to put it aside for a few days and then come back to it as though you had never seen it before. Alternatively, if there is no time for that, you might try doing something else – make some phone calls, meet some friends – and then come back to it. The psychological switch will probably help to create the required distance. Another technique is to read out loud what you have written, as *hearing* often reveals the difference between what you intended to say and what you actually did say. In the same way recording what you have written and then playing it back can also be very helpful.

Finally, do begin writing the easiest parts first. Now this may sound like such obvious advice that it may not seem necessary to mention it, but it is surprising how many people believe that a thesis (or anything else for that matter) should be written in the order that it will be printed and subsequently read. Not true. In an article entitled 'Is the scientific paper a fraud?', Medawar (1964) explains the process of writing up research as an exercise in deception. By this he means that the readers are deceived into believing that the research was conducted in the way it is described and the report written in the logical and sequential manner in which it is presented. He maintains that this is misleading and might be discouraging to others who wish to conduct research and write scientific papers, but who find that nothing ever happens quite as systematically for them as it seems to do for the experts.

All this was in 1964 but still does not seem to be generally acknowledged. So we are restating it here (as we did in Chapter 2) in order that you may consider writing up the Method section first. You do know what you did, and how you did it, so it might be a good way of getting started on the thesis, even though this chapter will come well into the body of the finished work. Alternatively you may prefer to start with the literature review, which is a safe way of reminding yourself of what has already been written about your topic. If you do start here, though, be sure to remember to go through it again at the end as you may find that some important new piece of information was omitted because it was published since your review.

Finally, it is useful practice in writing to use, from the beginning, the appropriate conventions of your discipline in footnoting and referencing. A range of conventions is used; for example, whether footnotes are encouraged, allowed or forbidden varies considerably across disciplines, and you need to follow the accepted convention for your discipline. If you don't know what that is, choose one of the leading journals in your subject whose articles you are quoting and follow them. If you are quoting from a range of journals using different conventions, choose the one you prefer and state at the beginning of your thesis that you are using the conventions of the *British Journal of X*. You should not mix conventions.

### Action summary

1 Ensure that the four elements of the PhD form (background theory, focal theory, data theory, contribution) are adequately covered in your thesis.
2 Do not make your thesis (i.e., report) any longer than it needs to be to sustain your thesis (i.e., argument).
3 Write your thesis in readable English, using technical terms as appropriate but avoiding jargon.
4 From the beginning, use the footnoting and referencing conventions of your discipline.
5 Take every opportunity to write reports, draft papers, criticisms of others' work, etc., during the course of your research. Do not think that all the writing can be done at the end. If you do avoid writing you will not develop the skills to write efficiently, or even adequately, for your thesis.
6 Write up your final thesis in the order which is easiest for you. It does not have to be written in the order in which it will be read. The Method section is often a good place to start.

# 7

# The PhD process

In this chapter we are going to consider two aspects of working towards your PhD. First we will discuss the psychological nature of the experience, placing emphasis upon the fact that it has a significant emotional component in addition to the recognized intellectual one. Secondly, the practical issues involved in managing the work in the time available will be analysed, including the vital role of setting goals and establishing deadlines.

## Psychological aspects

### Enthusiasm

Postgraduates begin the period of their research full of enthusiasm for their new undertaking. This changes during the time that it takes to complete the course. Research has shown that the main reason that initial enthusiasm diminishes is the length of time that has to be spent working on a *single* problem (Phillips 1980). In this chapter we will refer to interviews that were conducted with postgraduates over the three years of their PhD research in order to give the flavour of how they were feeling during the different stages being reported.

Freddy, studying industrial chemistry at a technological university, said that during the years of his research he had become more remote and detached:

> In the beginning I had to concentrate hard on what I was doing, it completely occupied my mind. In some ways I've got less enthusiastic, at first I was full of enthusiasm for work and work was going to be very important, but at the end other things gave me much more satisfaction.

In general the students early enthusiasm revealed itself in the form of overambitious estimates of what they could accomplish during the first year. As time went by and deadlines came closer they felt the stress of time constraints and the monotony of focusing on a particular problem for an extended period.

At first Adam (architecture) was very excited about the direction in which his work was taking him, but 'I have more enthusiasm than organization and I hope my supervisor will help me to decide what to do next.' Later on he found that writing helped him to organize his thoughts, but this meant that he could not explore all the avenues that had begun to open up for him.

### Isolation

Postgraduates discover towards the end of the first year what *not* to do for their PhD. Generally they have experienced disappointments in the amount of work they have managed to get done during this period and usually feel that they should be much farther ahead than they actually are. Some examples from students at the end of their first year illustrate this point.

Greg (history) said:

> I don't feel I've got very far after a year. I think I could have done more. I'm frustrated at not making as much progress as I hoped but don't know how I could have achieved more.

Adam (architecture) said:

> It's difficult to know how well I'm doing as I'm working well but progressing really slowly.

Charles (astronomy) referred to contact with others during the course of his work:

> Most of the time communication is artificial. Conversation is just polite, you do it all the time with people.

> Communication, if it's real, is more between two minds. So
> I don't think of conversation as communication any more.

Charles was dissatisfied with the amount and quality of his interactions with his supervisor. He also felt that he had very little in common with others in his department; in addition, he was not talking with anyone about his work. This resulted in a period of isolation, even though he shared a room with another postgraduate and came to the university every day. The lack of intellectual stimulation and exchange of ideas with either peers or supervisor eventually led to a loss .of interest in his topic, which he thought was of no importance or interest to anybody else. Once again, work slowed down almost to a standstill.

In Chapter 2 we mentioned that Diana (biochemistry) complained that she was working alone in a laboratory full of people who were working alone. Bradley (English) provided an alternative viewpoint with 'I'm utterly alone but don't feel isolated. I'm happy to get on in my own time.' Although one might think that Diana and Charles are less isolated than Bradley, for them the experience is one of total isolation; while Bradley's perception of spending so much time on his own is not as extreme as theirs, or for that matter Adam's. Some months later Bradley had changed his mind; he reported: 'Postgraduates are treated scandalously. We're not treated in any way as members of the academic community. The pleasures of isolation are wearing rather thin.'

Regardless of discipline, topic, or university the postgraduates interviewed were suffering from the effects of the social circumstances in which they were working rather than from the work itself. Nevertheless, the effect of these feelings was to dampen their initial enthusiasm and slow down their pace of work almost to nil.

*Increasing interest in work*

As students develop self-confidence and gradually become independent of their supervisors, so too do they become more involved with their work because of its own intrinsic interest. Once you have learned how to interpret the results of your own efforts you will find that you can grapple with problems as they arise instead of turning immediately to your supervisor for advice. Once this happens you will find that you become increasingly absorbed in the work that you are doing, and that the problem you are investigating demands more and more of your time and attention.

In fact Bradley explained that he needed to feel that he had rounded off a schedule of work in the three years and that it was this inner drive that had kept him going. At first he had 'gravitated into research because I couldn't think what else to do'. By the third year he said that his 'natural inclination' to do anything other than work hard on his research and complete the thesis had become much less pressing. The thesis had become one of the most important things in his life, but this had certainly not been the case in the beginning. He described 'a lot of chafing and inner rebellion' at the start of his three-year period of registration, and dissatisfaction with the department and with supervision. Gradually, although he still did not admire the way things were done, these external irritations grew less important as he became more and more absorbed in his work. He commented on the relationship between a lack of direction from outside and the development of his own personal autonomy.

### Transfer of dependence from the supervisor to the work

As students become more involved with their work, so there is a lessening of the need for external approval. Postgraduates gradually learn how to interpret the results of their efforts and this helps them to grapple with problems as they arise, instead of turning immediately to their supervisors for advice.

For example, Adam said toward the end of his three-year period of research: 'In the beginning I wanted immediate feedback and was afraid to ask. When I got it plus the confidence, I stopped working so hard and felt secure.' Here he is talking about the way that his own increasing independence in his work is related to a lessening of dependence on productivity. It is from the student's output that the supervisor is able to evaluate progress in the explicit terms necessary for giving feedback. Therefore, this comment from Adam indicates a simultaneous growth in independence from external approval coupled with reliance on the information he was receiving as he worked on his topic. The more he felt he could rely on his own judgement of the quality and standard of his work, and the longer he could develop his thinking, the less he needed to turn to his supervisor for comment, criticism or interpretation.

As Adam became his *own* supervisor, by evaluating his efforts without needing a third party to act as mediator between him and his work, he felt less pressure to produce something tangible to show Professor Andrews. This meant that, although it might appear that he was doing less, he was in fact working steadily without forcing himself to complete a piece of work before he was ready to do so, merely in order to be seen to be producing.

He may be compared to Ewan (nuclear chemistry) who did not continue to develop the confidence in his own work that was necessary if he was to be able to rely on the feedback provided through his own achievements – or lack of them. Near the end of his registration period Ewan said:

> I don't think that my early relationship with my supervisor was good and he wouldn't give me information first-hand. At first I had to do all the work without any lead, but later that changed. If you begin to enjoy the relationship with your supervisor then positive feedback is obvious. Some supervisors would opt for the student to dig up the research themselves; it would make you approach the problem differently and is a better training for later work when you have to cope alone.

Dr Eustace had started to supervise Ewan by referring to articles he should read but leaving him to develop his own thinking about the subject. Later he realized that Ewan needed more direction than the guidance that he had been giving and continued to increase the closeness of his supervision right up to the end of Ewan's period of registration. Ewan had been happy to depend on his supervisor but now commented on how the 'spoonfeeding' he had ultimately received had affected his work. He linked his considerable dependence on his supervisor with his lack of intrinsic work satisfaction and involvement. He was convinced about the importance of external control while, at the same time, being aware that his own training may not have been the most efficient for later autonomy in research.

These two examples describe quite different relationships between postgraduates and their supervisors, and differing perceptions of what they considered important to their progress. The examples also illustrate the importance placed on the need for information concerning their progress that the students expect to receive from their supervisors. Equally important, as the examples show, is the need for students to understand and accept the feedback that is constantly available in their own work.

At the end of his postgraduate days Ewan said: 'It's important to get good guidance, and I feel my supervisor is doing this.' But Dr Eustace, the supervisor, said: 'Following superhuman efforts to get sense into him, he's got experimental results as good as anyone.' In fact his supervisor continued to see Ewan weekly right up to the end of his period of registration. He edited, corrected and rewrote large sections of Ewan's thesis, and the student never did manage to discard his dependence completely and rely on the information which resulted from his own efforts.

## Boredom

About halfway through the period of research postgraduates tend to get 'fed up', confused and feel completely 'stuck'. This 'getting nowhere syndrome' has been remarked by Liam Hudson (1977b), who discussed it as part of his own experience of doing research. Supervisors too commented on it during the interviews. Professor Forsdyke (industrial chemistry) said of Freddy: 'During the next six months he'll get through the sticky patch and results should just pour out.'

Freddy himself reported, however: 'It's the boring part now, essential to the thesis, just plodding on. Just churning out results with no thought, no challenge.' Bradley said, philosophically: 'I see it's always darkest before dawn, it's just me and it [the thesis] now.' Adam said: 'Now that I know that what I'm doing is good enough for a PhD I've lost interest; there's no challenge.' Greg (ancient history) said: 'I'm really fed up with it right now, doing the mechanical things just goes on.'

The monotony and repetitiveness of concentrating on the same thing for an extended period of time are quite common. Both seem to be an integral part of learning how to be systematic about research and disciplining yourself to continue, despite the fact that everything seems eventually to become predictable if the work is proceeding as it should.

## Frustration

As the research progresses, new ideas about how to follow up the results of work that you have already done are constantly being generated. It is very tempting to pursue some of these new avenues, but if you are to complete the agreed research programme in time it is important to concentrate on the problem in hand and not be sidetracked. This becomes increasingly frustrating as the original problem becomes more and more familiar. Not being able to follow up results, ideas and theories is a constant source of dissatisfaction and frustration for most postgraduates at the end of their second year.

So do beware lest these common feelings and reactions against what might have become mechanical and repetitive work prevent you from continuing. It is only by understanding the need for precision and having the ability to apply yourself in a disciplined way that you will eventually get to the point where you have the right to follow up interesting leads and explore a series of ideas that arise out of the work in hand. We suggest that, for the moment, this should be *after* your doctorate.

In his autobiographical novel *The Search* (1958), C. P. Snow gives an excellent account of how he coped with the kinds of frustrations that result from a systematic programme of research. He explains that he spent years of his life doing 'bread and butter' work until he had made enough of an impact on the scientific community to enable him to undertake some fascinating but seemingly irrelevant research:

> I could not expect the authorities to take me as a rising scientist on trust. I had to prove myself . . . To begin with I was going to work on a safe problem. It was not exciting but almost certain to give me some results. [p. 55.] . . . With the future temporarily assured, I turned eagerly once more to the problem which had enticed me for so long. I had done enough for place and reputation and I could afford to gamble on what might be a barren chase . . . I had gained a good deal of experience and technique in research. [pp. 90–1.]

We cannot do better than offer those words of a well known and perceptive scientist as advice on how to approach the research you undertake for your PhD degree. Don't let your frustrations allow you to deviate. Remember that once you have your doctorate you will be in a far better position to experiment with your ideas.

## A job to be finished

In Chapter 3 we described the different ways in which research students talk about their PhDs as they come to the end of their period of registration. It seems to be important for the morale of most postgraduates that they think in terms of a goal – 'got to get it!' – or an unfinished task that needs completion – 'must finish!' You will recall that, by the time they were reaching the end of their period as research students, the postgraduates being interviewed realized that it was determination and application, rather than brilliance, that were needed to complete what they had started.

You will recall that in Chapter 2 we mentioned the way in which this idea of 'brilliance' inhibits the development of new postgraduates. Because they believe that people with a PhD are outstandingly clever, they admire those who have them – especially those in their own field whose work they have read. In the same way they do not see themselves as outstandingly clever and so are sure that they do not now, nor will they ever, merit the coveted degree. Once they are firmly embarked on their post-graduate career they gradually come to understand that the requirement is not for any outstanding abilities – other, of course, than those to do with persistence and overcoming feel-ings of boredom and frustration.

This realization is a step towards a changed perception of the PhD. It is necessary to come to the eventual description of research work as just that – work. If you have not managed to make this switch in the way you think about your research by your third year, do spend some time analysing precisely what it is that you realistically hope to achieve in your research. If you *have* got to the point of realizing that your work, just like any other kind of work, needs to be planned and developed and *com-pleted* in a given period of time, you will have entered the final crucial motivating state of the process. There is a job to be finished: the time has come when you must set a deadline for completion. As with other jobs, you will be rewarded at the end of it; not in this case by a financial bonus, but by a higher degree.

You will by now have become more skilled in the techniques and mental attitudes that this work demands. You will, too, have come to terms with the anxiety that all research students experi-ence. The most pervasive of all the psychological aspects of doing a PhD is the anxiety that accompanies you through all the stages. At first it is very high, and exemplified by such concerns as 'am I clever enough?', 'will ''they'' realize what a fraud I am?' and so on. As you progress, you go through periods of higher or lower anxiety but you are never completely free of it. It comes in bursts, and one of the reasons for feeling that a great weight has been lifted from you once you have successfully completed your PhD is that the nagging anxiety that has been your constant com-panion for so long has finally been lifted.

As your perception of the postgraduate situation changes you will find that your behaviour will adjust to match it. You will have discovered that you are *not* destroyed by criticism and that you have developed a new confidence in yourself, which will stand you in good stead in the oral examination. The job of work started so long ago is about to be finished; the end is in sight.

Now you are actively progressing towards this goal in a very matter-of-fact and routine manner. There are discussions to be held with your supervisor; writing to be completed; decisions to be made about which publications can be excluded and which *must* be referred to; final checking of statistical calculations or experimental results; a last look at data that have not yet been incorporated into the story you will be telling; and some theoretical concepts to be mulled over.

All of these are the loose ends that need to be tied up in order for the job to be ready for inspection. The aim is for your PhD to be a high-quality product.

## Practical aspects

### Timetabling and time management

The psychological aspects of the PhD process that we have just discussed develop continuously, often in recurring cycles, throughout the whole period of the research project. We now have to consider the conceptual and practical tasks which have to be undertaken to obtain a PhD. Since these have to be achieved within a limited period, timetabling and time management become crucial to success.

You will probably have three years full-time in which to design, conduct and complete your PhD, or an equivalent amount part-time, spread over five or six years. Of course, you will have some idea of what you will be doing during those years but how much thought have you given to just *how* and *when* you will be undertaking specific activities?

These activities operate at two levels: (i) the general level at which the tasks required to complete a PhD must be realistically charted if they are to be accomplished in the time available; and (ii) the detailed level concerned with setting timetable deadlines for particular tasks, and achieving them. In addition, the activities must be seen as both part of the research task *and* part of the essential structure into which the timetabling of the PhD falls.

At first you will have an overall plan such as that described by Ewan at the start of his research: in nuclear chemistry 'I hope eventually to come up with the *shape* of the molecules in solution'.

He was unable to be more specific than that but quickly discovered that before he could proceed several preliminary steps had to be taken. First he had to calibrate the viscometer that he would be using. In order to do this he had to read the literature on viscosity to see how such calibration had been done previously. Once he started to read, he realized that there was a confusion in the literature, which had to be sorted out. In order to do this he had to check the calculations reported in the journals; this involved engaging the help of a mathematician. Therefore, his overall plan could more accurately be described as: 'to find the shape of the molecule in solution by making measurements with a viscometer, calibrated according to verified equations'. This more sharply defined overall plan was gradually formulated as Ewan thought about what he had to do and began the work.

This is not an unusual situation. New postgraduates enter the system with a vague overall plan that will get them to their long-term goal of a PhD at the end of three years. Their short-term goals may be more clearly defined: starting work on the problem, discussing what they want to do with their supervisor and gaining access to equipment or samples. But beyond that, goals are very fuzzy indeed. This is because there is a tendency to take an unstructured approach to the project regardless of the time constraints and interim tasks to be undertaken and completed.

## The timetabling process

At first three years (or six years part-time equivalent) will appear to be an extraordinarily long time for completing a single piece of research. Beware of this illusion. If you trust it and behave accordingly you will be in very deep trouble later on. A postgraduate in biochemistry learned this the hard way. At the end of her second year of research into anti-cancer drugs, Diana said:

> I'm aware that I've only a year left and two years have already gone. Three years doesn't seem half long enough; it seemed a long time in the beginning. Now I'm trying to finish off groups of experiments and say 'that's the answer' rather than exploring it more fully, which is what I used to do.

The importance of not losing sight of the time constraints on each part of your project is clear.

It is useful to look on the total process as a series of tasks which lead to the *progressive reduction of uncertainty*. As we saw in

Chapter 5, there is a form to a PhD that structures the overall amount of work to be undertaken. This form generates a series of stages that have to be gone through. These stages, in turn, will point to a series of tasks that you will have to do. Going from 'form' to 'stages' to 'tasks' in planning what needs to be done becomes more and more specific to the individual research project and is an important part of your interaction with your supervisor (see Chapters 8 and 9). In principle, as you carry out each of the tasks that comprise the stages you should be reducing the uncertainty involved in your thesis. So you start with a wide field of possible topics and end, after some years of work, with the very specific report of your particular PhD research.

## The duration of the process

Overleaf is a suggested model for the form of the thesis and the stages of the process. The form, as we have seen in Chapter 6, is constant. The stages are fairly standard but there will be some variation according to your discipline. For the purposes of discussion the figure represents typical stages within the usual timescale for a PhD.

The figure is, and is intended to be, quite crude in that it uses timeblocks of 'terms' (i.e., four months of full-time work or six months of part-time work) and outlines only seven stages of the PhD process. However, it does illustrate the sort of programme that you will need to develop in conjunction with your supervisor. You need this framework in order to be continually aware of how your current work fits into the overall time allocated. Otherwise you will find, like Diana, that you wake up one morning to discover that half of your time has gone and you haven't 'really' started.

The aim of the exercise is to reduce the areas of uncertainty as we go from left to right along the timescale shown in the figure. At the overall level blocks of time are allocated to the background theory, focal theory, data theory and contribution elements of the thesis. More specifically, seven stages of the process are identified, the first six being allocated one 'term' each and the last stage (writing up) three 'terms'. In our experience this is a fast, but not unrealistic, timescale; some have achieved it, many fallen behind. An appropriate adaptation of this figure for you should serve regularly to locate your current work in the overall process, and therefore enable you to make realistic plans which motivate you to keep going until you have completed the work.

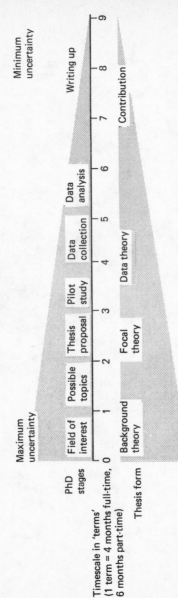

The PhD process
as the progressive reduction of uncertainty

Maximum
uncertainty

Minimum
uncertainty

| PhD stages | Field of interest | Possible topics | Thesis proposal | Pilot study | Data collection | Data analysis | | Writing up | |
|---|---|---|---|---|---|---|---|---|---|

Timescale in 'terms'
(1 term = 4 months full-time,
6 months part-time)

Thesis form

Background theory

Focal theory

Data theory

'Contribution'

An example of a time-based programme of work.  You need to develop an appropriate version for yourself in agreement with your supervisor.

Of course, it is unrealistic to expect that you will go through these stages in a straightforward, linear way. You may lag behind, you may have to revise earlier stages, you may have to jettison earlier work altogether and replace it, etc. This is all the more reason for keeping a time-based framework such as this.

## The stages of the process

Most of these stages will be relevant in some way to your work, although the detailed working out may vary. Some comments on them:

* *Field of interest.* The important point here is that the field should really be of interest to you. You are going to spend a lot of time saturating yourself in it over the next few years. It should have some intrinsic attraction for you to help along your motivation, since you need all the boosts that you can get.

  You may not be in a position to make choices about your field. This might come about because, for example, of the un-availability of apparatus or research sites. Then you have to work to kindle your interest in the area that *is* available to you. Through your own choice or enlightened recognition of necessity, you have to develop during this period a commitment to your field of work capable of carrying you through to the end.

* *Possible topics.* This stage is concerned with getting ideas that are worth researching and researchable in the time available. The fact that it is not until the next stage that a choice of the actual thesis topic needs to be made does not mean that you can float through *this* stage having no specific topics but only general ideas. Quite the opposite! You should be working up two or three topics in some detail to enable you to make a realistic professional choice at the next stage.

  You should be thinking of two or three research proposals, each about, say, four pages long. These should form the bases of discussions with your supervisor in which the two of you test out how viable they are in research terms, and how realistic in time terms. The capacity to spot worthwhile openings and fashion them into researchable topics is the key professional skill of the whole doctoral learning process, so practice at this stage is vital.

* *Making a thesis proposal (including the design of the investigation).* At this stage you are going to work in much greater detail to

establish that your proposed research investigation (a) will address the problem convincingly and (b) is likely to make a contribution. You will therefore need to examine the current focal theory quite fully and survey the background theory to estimate the likelihood of contributing.

A key point to bear in mind here is that an ideal design will involve 'symmetry of potential outcomes'. What this means is that ideally the thesis will not stand or fall by *a particular result*, but will be able to make a contribution whatever the outcome. Thus a high mean value or correlation will support one argument, while a low mean or lack of correlation will be equally interesting because it fits in with another line of approach. This symmetry cannot always be obtained, but it is worth exploring carefully to see whether you *can* obtain it. If present it is a great advantage in establishing at a later stage the contribution of the research work.

- *Pilot study*. The precise nature of this stage will vary considerably across disciplines. It may involve testing apparatus, data collection methods, sampling frames, availability of materials, etc. Essentially we are asking here: will it work?
- *Data collection and analysis*. The collection and analysis of data are activities clearly specific to each discipline and, within that, to each topic. One generalization that we would make, though, is that good researchers at this stage are very close to their materials. They know their raw data practically by heart, let alone the analytical results that are derived from them. They are in no sense 'laid back' but are living, eating and sleeping the stuff. This involvement is very important as it is the psychological basis that gives researchers the facility to see that data from different angles and in terms of different theories. It enables them – often unconsciously – to 'test' their material against new, innovative, offbeat ideas. They conceptually play with their data, intuitively trying lots of 'what-ifs', and often can come up with a new, interesting conception that makes a contribution to the subject.
- *Writing up*. For reasons already discussed in Chapter 4, the writing-up stage always takes longer than intended. A period of three 'terms' is not generous, even though it has been done in less (i.e., two 'terms') by determined and able students. Anything less than two terms full-time or a year part-time is quite unrealistic considering the nature of the task, which includes the 'contribution' component as described in Chapter 6.

## Redefining long-term and short-term goals

If you do not take this kind of structured approach to planning your PhD work, then one result will inevitably be a much greater dependence on your supervisor for feedback concerning your progress. Evaluating your own work will also be more difficult.

If you define short-term goals it will be less necessary to rely on external sources of information, such as supervisors, because the step-by-step structure will be clear. This clarity results in information on progress that you can interpret for yourself with very little difficulty. First, you will know whether you have managed to do what you said you would do; next, you will know whether you managed to do it in the time allocated. If – exceptionally, we must say – both these aspects of your work are as anticipated, then it is only the *quality* of the work that needs to be evaluated by your supervisor. In time you will be able to do this evaluation for yourself; but the best way of learning how to judge your own efforts is to pay careful attention to your supervisor's comments.

If, on the other hand, you discover that you have not managed to complete the projected work in the time assigned to it, you will be in a good position to analyse the reasons. You might estimate how much was due to circumstances that could neither have been foreseen nor prevented, and how much was due to your own inexperience, inactivity or inability to estimate the amount of work accurately. This last is the most usual discovery.

Typically, research students gradually realize that progress is slower than they had expected. This realization eventually leads to a reassessment of what may, realistically, be achieved. As this happens with short-term goals the related longer-term goals can be adjusted too. Once you know what it is you have to get done in the immediate future it will not matter so much that your more distant goals are rather fuzzy. As you progress through a series of related goals, either the long-term ones get closer or, if they do not, you rethink what you want to achieve.

Sometimes the rethinking results in the overall goal of the PhD being changed to that of an MPhil. This is usually both unfortunate and unnecessary. The decision is based on panic, unless, of course, the original selection was quite incorrect or the supervisor has completely neglected his or her own part in the undertaking. More often the rethinking results in a narrowing and redefinition of the research problem. When such a redefinition occurs, which involves coming to terms with the limitations of research for a higher degree, it is a very good sign that one important lesson has already been learned.

An example of such positive redefinition as a result of disappointment with progress toward short-term goals comes from Adam. At first he said that his thesis would deal with the problem of 'how to transmit the building rule system of a culture in a way that can be used to accommodate change'. He knew precisely which books to read and that only very few of them would be in architecture. But his reading and note-taking became much more extensive and took many months longer than he had anticipated, primarily because he became very interested in a structuralist approach to social anthropology and cognitive development. His thesis eventually became a contribution to the controversy raging in design education concerning whether the designer is a *tabula rasa* who 'creates' according to inspiration, or whether there is a starting point with an existing lexicon of known forms.

The redefinition was possible because Adam had set himself short-term goals of writing specific sections within set time limits. As he repeatedly failed to achieve these goals, he decided to look at the long-term goals in the light of what he had discovered during the course of his reading, writing and note-taking. In this way his thesis became redefined. If he had just continued with his research without any kind of monitoring in the light of pre-set constraints, he would inevitably have had a last-minute panic. He would then have had to decide whether to take a much longer time to complete his thesis or, alternatively, to put together whatever he had managed to achieve in the time available and hope that it would be adequate.

## The importance of deadlines

Where, you may ask, is the supervisor in all this? Well, of course, supervisors have a very important role to play in the negotiating and setting of short-term and long-term goals. However, many supervisors accept postponed appointments or long gaps between meetings with their research students without putting much effort into persuading them that they need a tutorial. This is often due to concern on the supervisors' part that they may be pressing their students and so causing undue stress. Sometimes it is because they assign too little importance to the task of supervision in comparison with their lecturing loads, developing their own research and keeping up their writing output.

It may be that the supervisors are not really aware of just how important it is to ensure that goals are set and deadlines met. Students need a goal closer than 'a thesis some time in the future', but not all supervisors realize that even good students often lack confidence.

Many supervisors have difficulty in understanding that their students find it hard to create and work within a structured time-table. It seems clear to the supervisor, particularly if the work requires a series of experiments or interviews, that there is a natural structure which it is straightforward to follow. But very often students are confused and cannot decide what to do next. Supervisors hesitate to take the initiative in setting up a pro-gramme of regular meetings where they believe that part of what characterizes successful PhD candidates is being able to organize and administer their own working pace.

Yet PhD students have supervisors because they need guid-ance and support. The relationship between them is the basis for a social approach to knowledge. What is often lacking is com-munication regarding expectations and needs, in fact anything relating to the *process* of doing a research degree. If you have followed the suggestions contained in Chapter 2 you will have already set up some kind of verbal agreement regarding the working relationship and the way in which you will each carry out your role. Such an agreement will lessen the ambiguity and confusion for both parties to this relationship and make it easier to discuss how to arrange meetings and the setting of deadlines.

Deadlines create a necessary tension between doing original work and reporting its progress, either orally or in writing. Very few people are able to work well without some pressure (either internal or external). Knowing that a deadline is looming is usually sufficient for most people to get on and do whatever it is they are supposed to do. In fact it is not at all unusual for people to leave things until the very last minute because they find it difficult to work well if they are not under pressure – a strategy not to be recommended. But neither is it desirable, when you have a long period of time in which to complete something, to have no steps along the way. Such a lack of structure in the task or its timing is not conducive to effective working.

For these reasons it is really quite crucial to ensure that you have firm deadlines all the time. As we have seen with both Ewan and Adam, deadlines met and left behind provide a valuable index of how realistic the longer-term goals are. As you move towards them, those once-distant deadlines become short-term goals.

In fact for some students deadlines are very real external constraints. For example, for many biology students the seasons set clear time limits to experiments, with a year's penalty for failure to observe them. For many students, though, the timing of the work that they have to complete is not marked except by the final submission of the thesis after three years. In such cases it is imperative that *pseudo-deadlines* are created.

Pseudo-deadlines are time limits accepted by the student as a motivating device. They may be set by your supervisor, agreed between you both, or set by and for yourself. Even if this last is the case you must ensure that you have somebody to report to once the deadline has been reached. The public commitment that you have set up in this way strengthens your motivation. It may be that a friend, colleague or relative will agree to help, but this should be only in order for you to take smaller steps than you have agreed with your supervisor. Your overall agreement with your supervisor must include provision for regular reporting meetings. While it may not always be necessary to provide a written report for such occasions, it is certainly advisable, as one of the most important things that you have to do during the course of your research degree is to keep writing.

Supervisors can help their students according to their rate of progress by introducing a kind of weaning process into supervision. This should take the form of a structured programme that gradually reduces the amount of contact as the postgraduate gets further into the work. First, short-term goals should be set by the supervisor and a date set for a tutorial meeting. Later students can be left to undertake a somewhat longer and more complex piece of work and the date set for a telephone conversation or letter reporting progress. At this time a date for a meeting should be confirmed. If it has to be moved from the tentative date originally set, the student must give an adequate explanation of why this should be. In the final stages the onus should be more on the student to initiate the contact than it was in the beginning, but the supervisor should still be aware of a responsibility to 'chase up' a student who does not seem to be keeping to the agreement.

Deadlines are as important for monitoring the development of thinking as they are for ascertaining that an agreed amount of reading or practical work has been completed. Whatever the short-term goals set, regular opportunities to discuss progress and exchange ideas are vital to the development of the project and the continuing enthusiasm of the research student.

**Action summary**

1 Be aware of the psychological stages that research students go through on the way to a PhD. Use discussion with your supervisor and peer support group to ensure that you do not get stuck at any one stage.

2 Construct, in conjunction with your supervisor, an overall time plan of the stages of your research along the lines of the figure shown on page 74. This will enable you to locate your work in a time frame. Use this time plan to monitor your overall progress, and thus motivate yourself to continue on course.

3 For each stage, construct a list of tasks that have to be carried out. This will enable you to monitor your detailed progress.

4 With this approach, you will be in a better position to redefine any short-term goals in the (frequent) event of progress being slower than expected. It may even be necessary to redefine long-term goals.

5 Deadlines are important. Set realistic deadlines and achieve them. If there are no external constraints acting as deadlines (e.g., nature of the research topic, conference paper, seminar presentation) then set pseudo-deadlines to report to your supervisor or a peer to act as a motivating device.

# 8

# How to manage your supervisor

In this chapter we shall be considering a series of strategies for handling the all-important student–supervisor relationship. The relationship is so crucial that students cannot afford to leave it to chance. It must be managed. If students are to do this well, they must understand what their supervisors expect of them. Once they have this 'inside information' they will be in a better position to develop the skills necessary to reduce any communication barriers and sustain the relationship for mutual benefit.

## What supervisors expect of their doctoral students

In a study, one of us (EMP) found the following set of expectations to be general among supervisors, regardless of discipline:

*Supervisors expect their students to be independent*
This is not as straightforward as it may at first appear. Despite the emphasis put on independence throughout the whole period of working for a PhD degree, there are still very important aspects of the process that demand conformity: conformity to accepted methodologies, to departmental and university policies,

to style of presentation, and to those things which your supervisor considers to be important. Your supervisor is in a powerful position with regard to your work and to your own progress through the system. For these reasons it is no simple matter to balance the required degree of conformity with the need to be independent. The difficulty is compounded when we remember that many postgraduates come directly from a university and from schools that encourage obedience. The problem was made explicit by Dr Chadwick when he spoke of his first-year research degree student in theoretical astronomy:

> Charles asks too frequently 'what do I do next?' I prefer a student to think for himself. He's not among the very best people we've had but his progress is reasonably satisfactory. The only slight hesitation I have about him is an indication of lack of original thought shown in an obedient attitude which results in his doing whatever I say.

Here we have a situation where the student needs to be given the structure necessary for organizing his work but the supervisor considers that to direct his student to such an extent would be making him too dependent. In this case Charles went to several members of staff in the department asking for their advice on what he should be doing. In an interview about his progress he said to the researcher:

> Nobody cares if you come in or you don't, if you work or you don't. There's no point in making any effort – it's important to have someone standing over you.

Charles was emphasizing the fact that, as he saw it, it was not necessary to do any work which was not being closely monitored. He needed more direction than his supervisor was prepared to give and wished to rely more on Dr Chadwick's assessment of his work than on his own judgement. Charles should have spoken more openly to his supervisor about his difficulties in becoming instantly independent in his new situation. Of course, this is easier said than done. First, a student has to identify the problem and, secondly, pluck up enough courage to raise the issue in discussion. (It might help to take this book in – opened at this page!) If Charles had managed to raise the subject a lot of unhappiness on the part of the student and disappointment on the part of the supervisor would have been avoided.

*Supervisors expect their students to produce legible written work*

Having actually written something you may well feel such a sense of achievement and relief that you want to get it into your supervisor's hands immediately – especially if you have already missed a deadline or two! However, it is no more than a matter of courtesy to take the time and trouble to present it properly. It is preferable to type it; if you cannot do this yourself then try to persuade a friend or relative to type it for you. Alternatively, you must spend the money that would otherwise have been allocated to some outing or other little luxury on having it professionally typed. It should, of course, be typed in double spacing to allow room for comments.

It is a very good idea for all postgraduate research students to learn to type. Using a word processor it is not difficult to teach yourself, since if you are composing at the machine, you do not have to be able to touch-type. We would recommend that you buy a word processor if you cannot get access to one through your department. Even at current costs it would be cheaper to buy one at the start of your studies and use it throughout than to pay for all the necessary typing. This skill will prove to be invaluable in your future career, even if you are eventually fortunate enough to be assigned your own secretary. However, if you are a woman postgraduate *never* admit to being able to type if asked.

There is nothing more irritating to a busy academic than to be expected to read through pages and pages of handwritten script. Not only does it slow down the task intolerably but it detracts from concentrating on the line of argument being developed, as the concentration is needed to decipher words and phrases. Sometimes illegible parts are skipped, so the supervisor can miss completely a major point that the student is attempting to justify. To add insult to injury – from the supervisor's point of view – the student will probably complain subsequently that the supervisor merely made a cursory and superficial reading of the document.

In addition, presentation is a very important aspect of both the final thesis and any interim conference papers or journal articles that you will wish to submit. Therefore, having the discipline to ensure that all written work leaves you in an acceptable form is good practice for the future and a necessary part of your training. Maximizing the time you spend with your supervisor and getting the best you can in the way of comments and suggestions from *any* readers of your paper are valuable rewards for having made the effort to present your ideas in an easily readable way.

### Supervisors expect their students to seek advice and comments on their work from others

Not only is this an excellent method of ensuring that you optimize the time spent in discussing your work with your supervisor – it is also a strategy for maintaining contact with others who are interested in you, your work, and how you spend your time. One of the major dissatisfactions with the lifestyle of a research worker is that nobody else either understands or cares about what the researcher is doing. This leads to almost complete isolation and a feeling that perhaps it isn't really worthwhile after all. An effective means for combatting this and, in addition, gaining helpful input into your work is to keep one or two other people in close touch with what you are doing.

These people can be other academics, research students with whom you form a self-help relationship of mutual exchange, or other significant people in your life. The best way of keeping them in touch with what you are doing is to talk about your work from time to time. Surprisingly, you avoid the risk of becoming boring and making your work dominate the relationship by offering drafts of written work for them to read and comment on. This has two benefits: it allows you to spend the rest of your time together on other topics of conversation and it boosts the morale of your readers to think that somebody who is doing a PhD values their opinions. What this means is that you must be pre-pared (and willing) to accept criticism from your peers and not only from your supervisor and others in more senior positions than you. Hopefully, the criticism will be constructive and you will be able to select from it those points which seem helpful. This might entail rethinking an idea, restructuring some para-graphs or generally clarifying items that you did not initially present well because of your close association with the draft.

If you choose your readers carefully you will probably find that you want to redraft some sections of what you have written, if not all, before giving it to your supervisor for comment and dis-cussion. By these means you will (a) achieve a relationship with, at the very least, one other person who will be able to talk coherently and knowledgeably with you about what you are cur-rently doing, and (b) offer work to your supervisor that has been trimmed and reworked to a more sophisticated level than your initial rough draft.

*Supervisors expect to have regular meetings with their
research students*

Regular meetings can occur daily, weekly, monthly, termly or
even half-yearly. The more frequent the meetings, the more
casual they are likely to be, helping to create a climate for discussion. Formal tutorial meetings are less frequent and need to
be prepared for on both sides. Usually supervisors expect to
meet with their research students every four to six weeks. It is a
good idea to discuss the frequency of meetings when you first
agree the kind of student–supervisor relationship you are going
to have. We have already considered (in Chapter 2) the advantages and disadvantages of more and less frequent meetings, so
you will realize the importance of ensuring that a principle is
established that is satisfactory for both your own and your supervisor's way of working.

Your supervisor has to fit tutorial meetings with you (and other
postgraduates) into what is probably an already full work
schedule. In order to be of most use to you, your supervisor will
have had to spend some time prior to the meeting thinking about
you, your research and any problems connected with it, reading
anything that you have written and preparing a focus point for
the tutorial. In order for you to get the best out of your supervisor
it is essential that you allow ample time between setting up the
meeting and the actual date. It is a good strategy to agree dates
for the next tutorial during the course of the previous one. It is
also important that you do, in fact, turn up at the appointed time
and date. If you are late it produces additional difficulties for the
meeting. Either it will be cut short or your supervisor will be
worrying about work that should be attended to but which is
being neglected because of the time given to you. If you cancel a
meeting at short notice the time and thought that your supervisor has already invested in it is wasted. Nor does it augur well
for your future relationship or the seriousness with which future
meetings will be treated.

A very important part of managing your supervisor is to set a
good example. If you find that your supervisor is not as exemplary as the above model suggests, you can provide encouragement by behaving in an exemplary way yourself. By doing so you
demonstrate that you expect tutorials to be well prepared and
treated with equal respect on both sides. You may even wish to
phone a day or two before the planned meeting to confirm with
your supervisor that everything is in order for it and to ask
whether there is anything else you should be thinking about or

preparing that may not have been mentioned previously. At the end of the tutorial, be sure that both you and your supervisor have noted in writing what has been agreed as the next stage of the work.

### Supervisors expect their research students to be honest when reporting on their progress

Supervisors are not idiots – at least, not many of them – and they are not fooled by 'absent' students who leave messages saying that everything is fine and they will soon be needing a meeting or sending in a written draft. Neither are they taken in by the student who does put in an appearance from time to time, talks volumes about work in hand, new ideas and the next steps about to be taken in practical work, and then disappears again, never submitting anything tangible in the form of precise figures, graphs, experimental results or, of course, written work.

If there is a problem, if you are blocked, if you have lost confidence, if you are experiencing domestic troubles of whatever kind, or if anything else at all is interfering with the continuation of your work, then *do let your supervisor know about it*.

### Supervisors expect their students to follow the advice that they give, when it has been given at the request of the postgraduate

Now this really does seem to be a most reasonable expectation, yet it is surprising how often it is contravened. For example, when Bradley asked whether his reading was going along the right lines, Mrs Briggs told him that he needed to know the romantic literature. She explained that it was not enough to know the area only through two writers. But Bradley decided to concentrate on four works and read them thoroughly and carefully, rather than 'following up a lot of leads at the same time'. He could not see the point of reading the works of other authors when his PhD was to focus on a specific work of a specific writer. In other words he had not received the answer he was hoping for when he requested the advice – and so ignored it!

### Supervisors expect their students to be excited about their work

If the student is not excited about it, who else will be? How can they expect to arouse anybody else's excitement, enthusiasm or even interest? When postgraduates are really excited about what they are doing it stimulates those around them. Not only the supervisor but others in the department become more animated. Excitement is infectious. It works to the advantage of the student concerned if other people want to know what is happening and encourage conversation about the research. It is invigorating to be at the centre of a whirl of energy and enthusiasm. There is a world of difference between working away for the sake of getting on with something, in an environment where there is little communicable interest in what is happening, and wanting to tackle the next task from a desire to push ahead and let everyone else know about your progress.

Of course, there is a line to be traversed here between becoming unbearably boring and pompous about what you are doing and maintaining that element of excitement that keeps curiosity and the will to go 'just a little bit further' continually alive. If you succeed in maintaining this level of motivation then not only will your postgraduate days be full of enjoyment and anticipation but you will also have a head start in managing your supervisor to fit in with your own ideas of how the relationship between you should operate.

*Supervisors expect their students to be able to surprise them*
This stems from the fact that, if you are to be successful, it should not be too long before you know more about your area of research than your supervisor does. To be awarded a PhD means that you must become expert in your research topic. Therefore, although your supervisor is an expert in closely related areas, such expertise will fall short of the depth and detail on your own topic that you yourself are now developing. For these reasons your supervisor will expect to be constantly surprised by new information, evidence and ideas that you are able to supply.

Supervisors do *not* expect to be shocked by their students' failure to conform to a professional code of conduct, or falling short of a moral approach to their research and/or research subjects. So, to manage your supervisor successfully, be sure that you manage to steer the course between surprising them and shocking them.

*Supervisors expect their students to be fun to be with!*
Perhaps you think this is asking too much, but just think how much more enjoyable your own work is when you actually like the people with whom you are working. It has been said that anyone can become interested in any research topic, provided it

is within the broad area of general interest and knowledge of the individual concerned. But three years is a very long time indeed to spend with somebody who makes you feel ill at ease in any of a variety of ways. In other words, it is wiser to select your research topic to match the supervisor of your choice than to select your topic and then be paired with the relevant academic specialist. Just as you may take an instant dislike to somebody so, too, may your supervisor. It may not be as extreme as that of course, but doing a PhD is an intense and emotional experience that continues over a very long period of time.

What this means in interpersonal terms is that any irritant, no matter how minor it may appear in the beginning, becomes exaggerated and distorted over time until it is well nigh intoler-able. This works in both directions, so the supervisor's expec-tation of enjoying the time spent with you has its payoff for you too. It is not that you have to spend your time thinking up witti-cisms and novel ways of entertaining supervisors, in the hope of being invited to spend more of your out-of-work time with them and their social group; it is merely that it is advisable to follow the instructions given in Chapter 2. If you have selected a supervisor carefully and discussed the way that the supervisory relationship will work, then you have a head start over those who have not gone to this trouble.

Like any relatively long-term relationship, the one that you have with your supervisor will change over time. If you begin cautiously then you will increase the probability that the two of you will gradually grow to appreciate each other and so get to the point where you might even discover that you too expect your supervisor to be fun to be with. You might even find that, in working well together, you may manage to have fun too.

## The need to educate your supervisor

We have already discussed the importance of keeping your supervisor informed of new developments and findings as your work advances. Earlier in this chapter we mentioned that you will gradually become more expert, better informed and perhaps more skilled in specific techniques methods and areas of investi-gation than your supervisor.

Managing your supervisor efficiently involves an educational programme as well as a training course. The training course involves fulfilling the expectations of supervisors and moulding them to fit with your own needs and requirements. The educational programme need not be so subtle, as it is more acceptable to acknowledge that you will know more than your supervisor about your research topic, given time, than it is to admit that you have a supervisor who does not know how to supervise effectively. Nevertheless, it is recommended that you enhance the education programme by presenting information to your supervisor in as surprising and stimulating a manner as you can, thus maintaining an optimum level of excitement about your findings. All this will help to make you fun to be with too!

So much for the style. The content is important and not quite as uncomplicated as it may at first appear. You might find yourself in murky waters if you assume too little knowledge on the part of your supervisor or, alternatively, if you show that you have realized from your discussions that there are gaps in your supervisor's knowledge of the specialist field. It is fine to mention any new findings that are a direct result of your research, and, indeed, they *must* be mentioned in order to demonstrate the progress that you are making. Any readings or discussions with others that teach you something you did not previously know may also be mentioned easily to your supervisor. But beware of doing this in such a way that it becomes clear that you believe that your supervisor was also unaware of this information. In other words, it may be necessary to educate your supervisor by giving information in a manner that assumes that your supervisor already knew about the things that are only now becoming accessible to you.

Such measures will become less necessary as time passes and your own work becomes more advanced. You will find, if you have handled the situations described here sensitively, that your relationship with your supervisor has changed from one in which the supervisor is guiding or directing your work to one where *you* are in control of what you are doing. Instead of being someone from whom you need information and approval, he or she gradually becomes someone with whom you can discuss new ideas and develop your thinking. You will be more inclined to use your supervisor as a sounding board, as an expert with the ability to proffer the reverse argument to be countered. Instead of a teacher the supervisor becomes a colleague and the relationship becomes less asymmetrical than it was. In fact, this is the central aim towards which your relationship with your supervisor should be working.

It may be that you will have specialized in a particular technique or method so that your supervisor will not be able to test or replicate your investigations without considerable new learning and practice. It will then be more likely that your own findings and results will be accepted as correct, even if they seem doubtful, than would otherwise be the case. In such circumstances your reasoning as to *why* you think you should have got these results becomes an important focus in your discussions. Your interpretation of the evidence will also have to stand up to very strong inspection. All this is to the good because it gives you practice in arguing your case, which is an essential skill both for your viva and for any conference papers and seminars that you give on the topic. The learning that goes on in such a situation is very much two-way. You learn from your supervisor what kinds of questions are important and how to respond to them; your supervisor learns from you about the new methodological development and how it might be expected to affect the discipline.

Once your supervisor sees that you have confidence in what you are doing and begins to respect your work, it will become easier for you to educate him or her. Supervisors do benefit from having postgraduate students and they are aware of the role these students have in keeping them, the busy academics, in touch with new developments and at the forefront of knowledge in their field. All you have to do to keep your supervisor in a position to be of help to you throughout the whole period of your research is to ensure that he or she is aware of what you are discovering, more or less as you are discovering it.

If you are at this stage and feel that your supervisor is not taking your work as seriously as you would wish in giving comments, a good tactic is to ask whether the report, etc., warrants presentation in a conference paper. This makes it more likely that the work will then be fully evaluated.

## How to reduce the communication barrier

It should be clear by now that it is necessary for you to educate your supervisor to become the kind of person that you find it easy to talk to. It should also be clear that there are a variety of ways in which you can begin to do this. Some of them have already been mentioned but now let us look at them a little more closely.

It is first necessary to realize and remember that there is usually a difference between what supervisors actually do and what their students believe them to have done. For example, the time that supervisors allocate to their students includes time given to *thinking* about you, the student, as well as the obvious time allocation needed for reading what you write and the tutorial meeting.

It is important to show that you are aware of these things and appreciate the hidden time and effort that your supervisor gives to you. Showing your appreciation of this will make it easier for you to talk to each other more frankly, not merely gearing the conversation to purely technical matters. In fact, all too many supervisors feel that they need to keep closely in discussion to the actual work, thus avoiding the all-important PhD process, which includes your relationship. They may not have any experience of discussing openly and freely what they perceive to be 'personal matters'.

An example of this comes from Professor Andrews and Adam. The supervisor said of their tutorial meetings, 'He always seems to go off in a more contented frame of mind than when he arrives', but Adam reported, 'I haven't found a way of telling him how very frustrated I am with these meetings.' Here we have misunderstanding and a clear breakdown of communication between them. The misread signals resulted in the student being unable to follow any advice that he was given. This is partly due to the student's disappointment that Professor Andrews did not say what he, Adam, wanted him to say but merely assumed that everything was in order between them. If Adam had been better at managing his supervisor he would have told the professor how he felt, which would have opened up the way to a more honest and trusting relationship between them.

The most basic lesson to be learned in managing your supervisor is the necessity of encouraging very broad-ranging discussions. By doing so you reduce the communication barrier. It is necessary in almost every case to clarify misunderstandings of all kinds. The  way to get your supervisor talking about what may be perceived as 'taboo topics' is to ask direct, but positively constructed, questions revealing that you are assuming good intentions on their part. It is always a good idea to start from a general question that is not focused directly on the actual work, but neither should it be too personal too soon. For example:

Am I making enough use of the learning opportunities available?

Do you think that I am managing to get enough work done in the time between our meetings?

Are you satisfied with how I use your comments?

Are you satisfied with my attitude towards your supervision of me?

How do you think we might work together more effectively?

Such a series of questions should lead naturally into a conversation about the relationship itself. If supervisors do not feel unfairly judged, they will be more open. There will be no need for either of you to use defensive tactics, such as hiding behind technical details.

A further component in reducing the communication barrier with your supervisor was described in Chapter 2. Discussing your expectations and hopes for the working relationship between the two of you is of prime importance. If you agree an informal 'contract' that includes the amount and type of contact that would be acceptable at different times during the course of the work, you will have an effective basis for discussing any deviations. Your needs change over time, so part of the contract should be an agreement to review at agreed intervals, probably annually. With such a contract it is also easier for either party to request a change if the relationship is not working well.

In Chapter 7 we talked about the importance of deadlines. Here again is an important step in managing your supervisor. You must ensure that every time you leave a tutorial meeting there is another one agreed and written into the diaries of both of you. It is less important how near or far into the future the next meeting is; what is vital is that a date should have been fixed on which you know that you have to face your supervisor again.

We have seen how essential it is for you to receive constructive criticism; so do make sure that when the date fixed for a meeting arrives you help your supervisor to make the most of the time available. Once again, ask the right questions for eliciting the information that you need. If your supervisor says 'This section is no good', you should respond – tactfully, of course – with 'what *precisely* is wrong with it?' It may be that the grammatical construction is unacceptable; or that the conceptual design is misleading or confused; or that the section is irrelevant; or any of a dozen other things. You have to establish exactly what it is that is being criticized and what you can do about it to put it right.

You may need to omit the section completely, or move it to another part of the report, or rewrite it, or rethink it before rewriting it. You must help your supervisor to express clearly, and with as much information as possible, what it is that is wrong. Once you have the information you will be in a position to do something about it. You might want to discuss it further, and perhaps disagree; or persuade your supervisor of the correctness of the point you were trying (but apparently failed) to make; or go off and do whatever has been agreed between you.

It may even be necessary for you to help your supervisor to understand what doing a PhD means to you. In Chapter 3 we described how Mrs Briggs thought of a PhD. She contrasted it unfavourably with writing a book; she thought of it as preparation only for becoming a university teacher, and as creating artificial problems to concentrate on for a minimum of three years. However, as we have explained, a PhD is a thorough training in doing research and learning the criteria and quality required for becoming a full professional in a chosen field. It admits the holder to a club in which you are recognized as an authority and accepted as a person who is knowledgeable enough in a specialized area to be able to extend the boundaries of the subject when necessary. Doing a PhD is a hard training ground for a specific profession.

In this respect it might be a good supervisor management strategy to suggest that regular seminars be established within the department, in which you and other postgraduates can discuss your ideas for your research and the problems encountered *en route*. You could reassure your supervisor that it will not entail a great deal of additional work, as you and the other postgraduates will handle the administration. You will be seen as a person of initiative and ideas and high motivation. In addition it will make it easier for you and your supervisor to talk to each other on subjects not directly connected with the minutiae of your research.

Finally, if you want to succeed in managing your supervisor, you have to ensure that you do not make excessive demands and become a nuisance. Always speak honestly about anything that is bothering you and be direct in your requests and your questions. Take the responsibility for keeping the lines of communication open, because it is you who have the most to lose when misunderstandings and communication breakdowns occur. Try to make the relationship with your supervisor as far as possible a shared, if inevitably asymmetrical, partnership.

## Changing supervisors

It may be that you will feel that the relationship with your supervisor is not developing satisfactorily, and you might therefore consider changing. We are not referring here to situations where it becomes necessary to change supervisors for extraneous reasons (for example, your supervisor leaves the university) but situations in which you wish to initiate a change.

There is usually a formal mechanism that allows for the possibility of such a change, but it cannot be emphasized too strongly that this is a course not to be undertaken lightly. In the very early period of the research, during the first few months of establishing more precisely your common areas of research interest, an obvious mismatch of interests can often be rectified with relatively little difficulty. But a change made after that period, or made for any other reason, requires considerable heart-searching.

A change of supervisors is the academic equivalent of getting a divorce. There are the formal (legal) mechanisms for doing it but the results are achieved, inevitably, only after considerable emotional upset. There are important consequences for the supervisor's professional status and self-esteem if a student initiates a change. Thus it is bound to be a difficult process – often ending with metaphorical blood on the walls.

The important key to the process is to find and make use of a third party as a mediator. There should be such a person available. It might be the Sub-dean for Research, the Convenor of the Doctoral programme, the Chair of the Higher Degrees Committee, or the Research Tutor – the title will vary, but it will be a person who takes some responsibility for the system of doctoral supervision as a whole. If there is nobody specifically allocated to this task, then it is always possible to approach your head of department, who has overall responsibility for the academic working of the department.

The importance of the third party is in helping to improve communication so that both you and your supervisor get a better understanding of the problems. This role is also vital to finding ways of getting your current supervisor to accept a change, if that turns out to be necessary, without feeling too damaged by it. The third party is also essential for offering advice on, and making preliminary contact with, a new supervisor. The relationship between your old and your new supervisors, as departmental colleagues, will be preserved more easily with the help of the third party.

As an example, let us consider Nick. He was interested in working in a certain field of management operations in which research is not yet well developed. In his first year he attended seminars given by doctoral students across the whole range of management research. After some months he began to feel that his supervisor, Dr Newman, was not really directing the advice she was giving him to the sort of research approach he observed in his colleagues. It was far more discursive and descriptive than the analysis his peers were engaged in. Dr Newman on the other hand, felt that Nick was neglecting her advice on how to proceed, because he did not want to put in the groundwork to make himself knowledgeable about the field. In her view this was more important than the methodology.

Like so many students and supervisors in their position, they carried on for the whole of the first academic year with this uneasy relationship: Nick thinking that Dr Newman didn't *really* understand research, and she thinking that Nick didn't *really* want to do research that was worth doing in relation to her field. Towards the end of the year, the director of the doctoral programme became aware of this mutual dissatisfaction, and in discussion with both of them the possibility of transfer to another supervisor was considered.

Dr Newman believed that Nick would never carry out any research in her field anyway, so somebody else might as well have him. The proposed new supervisor was prepared to take him provided Nick was willing to start again from the beginning. The change was accomplished because the third party took the initiative in making all three aware of the relevant issues. Nick had lost a year in getting it all sorted out, but did indeed eventually obtain his PhD in the new field. Even so, Nick and Dr Newman avoided each other for the remainder of his time as a research student.

Monica, doing research into computer systems analysis, is another example of the difficulties involved in changing supervisors. She was so unhappy with the supervision she had received that, when asked about it a year after having gained her PhD, she started to cry and had to struggle to find the words to describe her feelings. She said:

> I knew that if I did the higher degree it would be difficult to get through it and that I needed a certain type of person – someone with a lot of grit – to supervise me. Dr Montague's a nice person outside of his role as supervisor but he wasn't

the right kind of person for me. The personal relationship between us was never established. I've blotted out most of this period except the pain.

Monica never felt that her work was taken seriously by Dr Montague. He saw her for tutorials only in his own home, with his children demanding attention. His comments were always supportive, and she felt that he was not being helpful by sparing her any criticism. Nor did he offer her any suggestions which she could build on.

Clearly some exercise of assertiveness would have been useful in this situation. Monica could have said quite unequivocally that she would appreciate it if Dr Montague would arrange to see her in his office during working hours, so that he could discuss her work privately. She could also have asked him direct and detailed questions as to how her work could be improved.

In fact, Monica eventually adopted an additional unofficial supervisor whom she felt *would* take her thesis work seriously. Dr Montague made no comment on this. It happened that the other academic was the acting head of the department and encouraging all research initiatives. After this relationship had continued for about 18 months the change of supervisors was formalized by the university.

## The perils of joint supervision

It may be, because of the interdisciplinary nature of your research field or the particular focus of your research topic, that joint supervision is proposed. Having more than one supervisor may seem like a good idea at first; after all, two or even three academics, instead of just one, will be involved in your research studies. In fact there are considerable perils in joint supervision, and it should be undertaken only if unavoidable and if considerable care is given to its operation.

The problems stem from:

- *Diffusion of responsibility*. It is paradoxically worse rather than better, to have two supervisors rather than one. There is a considerable likelihood that each supervisor will regard the other as taking the lead and having more of the responsibility. Even if this feeling is only subconscious, as it may well be, it acts to reduce the commitment of both of them. On the other hand, there have been cases where the supervisors use the student in order to score points off each other in their own power struggles.

- *Getting conflicting advice.* It is an unfortunate fact of life that the probability of seeing both your supervisors *at the same time* is considerably less than that of seeing them separately. They almost certainly will not have had a chance to confer together beforehand, so getting conflicting advice becomes a regular occurrence. If the conflict is not major, the commonest way out for the student is to do what *both* suggest, in the end doing considerably more work and delaying the progress of the project.
- *Playing one supervisor off against another.* But it is not only the supervisors' behaviour that might lead to problems – you, the student, also have a dangerously seductive avenue available. If you feel frustrated, alienated, trapped into doing something not of your choosing, then you can spend (waste) a lot of time and emotional energy playing off one supervisor against the other.
- *Lack of an overall academic view.* Probably the most important difficulty associated with joint supervision is that there is less likely to be one person who is willing to take an overall view of the thesis. Who will evaluate and criticize it as a whole in the same fashion as the external examiner? The weight of the necessary self-evaluation that the student has to do is therefore considerably increased.

For all these reasons, joint supervision is not to be recommended as a first choice. In addition we would emphasize that having a single supervisor does not in any sense mean that you cannot have access to the expertise of other academics for particular aspects of your work. You can, and certainly should, go to them for help, advice, criticism as often as you need them. Your supervisor is not going to object as long as you make sure that he or she hears about all the discussions and developments which you are undertaking.

The advantages of a single supervisor stem basically from the commitment that such a relationship generates, combined with an overall view of the thesis. These are crucial. If you are in a situation where joint supervision appears to be inescapable, a possible way of coping is to get agreement on the unequivocal division of the areas of responsibility between them. Better still, try to get some of these benefits by establishing that you have a first supervisor who takes the lead and a second supervisor who gives support – as in the CNAA system – rather than two equals.

## Action summary

1  Be aware that you must accept the responsibility for managing the relationship between you and your supervisor. It is too important to be left to chance.
2  Try to fulfil the expectations that supervisors have of their students. If you cannot fulfil any of these expectations do not neglect them, but raise the issues in discussion.
3  You need to educate your supervisor continually. First, on the research topic, in which you are fast becoming the expert. Second, on ways of understanding how the supervisory role can best help in your own professional development.
4  Look for ways of reducing the communication barrier between you and your supervisor. In addition to research content, discuss at various times working relationships, setting deadlines, what doing a PhD means to you, the adequacy of provision for research students, and so on.
5  Ensure that every time you leave a tutorial you have agreed and noted down a date for the next one. Be punctilious in meeting appointments and deadlines, so that your supervisor will be too.
6  Help your supervisor to give you better feedback on your work. Always ask supplementary questions to ensure that you understand fully what is being required of you.
7  If you are seriously considering changing supervisors, use an appropriate third party as a mediator.
8  If you have to have joint supervision, ensure that there is a first supervisor and a second supervisor, rather than two supervisors with equal responsibility.

# 9

# How to supervise

This chapter is principally addressed to supervisors. We shall be considering a series of strategies for improving supervision. It will help you identify aspects of the role that you may not previously have considered. But this chapter will also give students some insights into the tasks of their partner in this enterprise, thus helping to improve the quality of the relationship on both sides.

For supervisors to improve their performance, they must understand what their students expect of them. Once they have this 'inside information' they will be in a better position to develop the skills necessary to teach the craft of research, maintain a helpful 'contract' and encourage students' academic role development. They will also be in a position, should this prove necessary to modify these student expectations to make them more appropriate to their particular situation.

## What students expect of their supervisors

In the study referred to in Chapter 8, Phillips (1980 and 1987) found the following set of expectations to be general among students regardless of discipline:

*Students expect to be supervised*

This may sound like a truism but it is surprising how widespread is the feeling among postgraduates of *not* being supervised. For example, Julia, interviewed a year after gaining her PhD in education, was still indignant at the limited help she had obtained from her supervisor. Dr Johnson had arranged to see her only irregularly – indeed there was one period of over six months during which they did not meet. While he made detailed comments on work that she presented, he never discussed with her the overall shape of the study, and as a result she spread her work too widely and thinly. Her research was concerned with mothers' attitudes to breast-feeding, and she tried to encompass both a library-based historical and anthropological study and a detailed attitude survey across two NHS regions.

There was clearly a limit to what she could do, but she felt that she had made a reasonable attempt to cover the whole topic. When she submitted her thesis, it came as a shock to her when the examiners at the oral examination said that she had tried to do too much and that neither component was adequate. On her resubmission, she was told, she should jettison the historical and anthropological work and concentrate on bringing the survey work up to the appropriate standard.

Dr Johnson had not suggested this before, although *after* the oral he was adamant that this was the thing to do. Julia's view is that he had just not given enough thought to the PhD and had therefore not been able to supervise her adequately. Dr Johnson's view was that if Julia had been good enough she *would* have been able to encompass both aspects of the topic. His supervision was properly directed towards that end until it became clear on the presentation that a different approach was required.

This is an extreme case, but such inadequacies of communication between supervisor and student are not unusual. Dr Johnson should have taken responsibility for ensuring that regular meetings were taking place between himself and Julia. He should also have taken care that these meetings included detailed discussions of the whole project so that he would know whether she was covering adequately the amount of work that they had agreed between them. Most importantly, he should have been supervising her writing by seeing early drafts of the whole thesis. If he had done this systematically he would never have permitted her to get to the point of a final draft that did not appear to be comprehensive enough in all areas of the work undertaken. Finally, the thesis should not have been submitted in the form that the examiners saw, because Dr Johnson should have informed his student that it was not likely to be passed as it stood.

More subtly, the feeling of not being well supervised can derive from the fact that students define the concept of 'supervision' quite differently from supervisors. For example, Freddy and Professor Forsdike (industrial chemistry) disagreed about the amount of time spent in supervising Freddy's research. Freddy said: 'He really oversupervises, he's in twice a day to see what results I've got.' But Professor Forsdike insisted: 'We don't meet as often as we should, about once a month only.'

What was happening was that Freddy counted every contact with his supervisor in the laboratory as a meeting, while the professor thought only of the formal tutorial appointment as contributing to supervision. What is more, Professor Forsdike reported that Freddy had plenty of ideas and that it was very much a shared meeting. This is very different from thinking merely in terms of 'keeping tabs on results', which is how Freddy interpreted his supervisor's role.

In fact Freddy continued to feel oppressed throughout the three years of his PhD research. He said: 'I feel just another pair of hands for my supervisor. No matter what I do there's always more. I still see him twice a day and he's still on my back trying to get me to do more practical work – but I won't.' However, Professor Forsdike assumed that Freddy needed his support for as long as the postgraduate was prepared to accept it. If the two had talked to each other about this situation it could have been resolved at a very early stage, instead of continuing, as it did, almost to the end of the three years. There are, in fact, two different types of meetings. One type is minor and frequent and part of the continuing relationship. The other type is less frequent and more formal, and needs preparatory work on both sides. The difference in purpose needs to be made explicit.

*Students expect supervisors to read their work well in advance*
From the students' point of view it may appear that the supervisor has read only a little of the work submitted, at the last minute, and wishes to discuss it in the minimum time possible. Often students' only previous experience of receiving feedback on written work has related to undergraduate essays. They expect comments to be written on the script and to include an overall evaluation. Their idea of a tutorial is to discuss in detail all

the points made by the supervisor. But this is not necessarily the best way to set about commenting on work, whether it is a progress report, a description of recent experimental or other research work, or a draft for a section of the thesis.

Most supervisors prefer to focus on specific aspects of the students' work and discuss these in detail. This is because they wish to discourage their students from straying too far from a particular line of research. By ignoring the related, but irrelevant, issues raised by postgraduates they hope to communicate their satisfaction with those areas of concern which should be developed. At the same time they trust that this strategy will dampen the enthusiasm of those students who are sidetracked into exploring all kinds of interesting ideas which will not further the progress of the research or the thesis.

However, this way of dealing with written work can lead to considerable bad feeling and a breakdown of communication between students and supervisors. The following quotation illustrates the problem as it was experienced by Adam and Professor Andrews (architecture):

> [Adam:] After seven weeks of writing he only talked about a very minor aspect of my paper. I realize now that my supervisor is not going to be of any help to me. He doesn't read what I write, so I've realized I'm going to have to get on without him.
>
> [Professor Andrews:] Each time I choose a single aspect from a paper he has written and suggest that he develops it, I see his work evolving and developing very satisfactorily.

Yet Adam was not at all sure whether he was on the right track and he was unclear about what it was that he was supposed to be doing. It is here that it is essential that communication is clear between the pair. Commenting on work submitted by a postgraduate student means talking around it. The script should form the basis for a discussion. Its function should be to further the student's thinking about the project through an exchange of ideas with the supervisor. The script may be put away and used later as an aide-memoire for the thesis, parts of it may even be included as it stands. But it is *not* a complete and final piece of work in which every word merits detailed attention. It is the task of supervisors to make clear to their students how they intend to use written work to further the research.

*Students expect their supervisors to be available when
needed*

It is true that the majority of supervisors believe that they *are*
always ready to see any of their students who need them, but
there are many who are not quite as available as they believe
themselves to be. It is good practice for supervisors regularly to
take coffee or lunch with their students – or to buy them a drink
– in order to facilitate easy communication.

A major reason for lack of availability among those supervisors who have secretaries with adjoining offices is the loyalty
with which their secretaries protect them from the outside
world – especially from students. Even if the secretary has
been told that research students may make appointments
whenever they wish, the postgraduates themselves may have
difficulty in going through this formal channel to ask their
supervisor something that might be considered quite trivial.
The result of this can be long periods without working and
with increasing depression on the part of the student who is
afraid of bothering the busy and important academic. On the
other hand this situation engenders frustration on the part of
the supervisor, coupled with doubt about the student's motivation.

Even when supervisors do not have secretaries keeping
guard in an outer office and maintaining their appointments
diaries, postgraduates still find it difficult to initiate an
unplanned meeting – especially if it means having to knock on
a closed door.

Sheila found that if she met her supervisor as they were walk-
ing down a corridor, or across the campus, she had difficulty in
getting beyond the superficial exchange. Requesting a tutorial in
these circumstances seemed to be inappropriate, in case the
supervisor was in a hurry to get to a meeting or give a lecture.
There have even been cases where students and supervisors
have travelled a few floors together in a lift and the student has
still been unable to say there is a problem or that a meeting is
needed. Supervisors ought to be sensitive to these difficulties
and ensure that regular meetings are maintained.

When supervisors make it clear that they do not welcome
impromptu meetings with their students because of the weight
of other commitments, it becomes almost impossible for many
students ever to pluck up enough courage to request a tutorial.
This means that a student who gets 'stuck' has to waste time
waiting for a meeting arranged by the supervisor.

*Students expect their supervisors to be friendly, open and
supportive*
In Chapter 2 we referred to the difficulties experienced, even by
mature postgraduates, in informal social contact with their
supervisors. We also pointed out the supervisors' ignorance of
these difficulties. In this chapter the focus is on the more formal
aspects of the relationship.

Many of the same tensions are present. Supervisors often feel
that if they have established an easygoing, first-name relationship, their students will perceive them to be friendly and open.
However, as we have seen, this is not necessarily the case. For
example, Charles, who was doing a PhD in astronomy, said:

> It's very difficult to prise things out of Dr Chadwick, so I'm
> not sure if this meeting today will result in a big step for-
> ward for my research. Our meetings are rather silent
> affairs, as I wait for him to prompt me and he gives very
> little feedback and only chips in from time to time. I don't
> get much help, information or encouragement from him. I
> know that he *is* my supervisor and I don't want to slight
> him, but I seem to be avoiding him at present.

Here, Charles is expressing dissatisfaction with tutorial meetings to the point of trying to keep out of view of his supervisor.
This made life particularly difficult, as they had rooms just along
the corridor from each other.

Dr Chadwick, however, still felt that things between them
were reasonably satisfactory:

> Our relationship is friendly, even though I never see him
> outside the formal interview situation. Our meetings are
> irregular but fairly often, about once every two or three
> weeks, usually at his initiative. They last up to half an hour
> but could be as little as 15 minutes. Most of the time we
> meet to consider details of the computer program he's
> working on, so he has to explain the nature of the problem
> and then we discuss it. These programs will be used a lot
> and so have to be very efficient.

It is clear that Dr Chadwick does make himself available when
Charles requests a meeting and takes it as a sign of success that
Charles asks to see him. Although Charles avoids using Dr Chadwick's name when talking to him, the fact that he brings problems
along confirms his supervisor in his belief that he is being
friendly, open and supportive. Unfortunately, Dr Chadwick is

totally unaware of Charles's inability to talk to him about research matters which are bothering him. An effective supervisor, on the other hand, would not merely stick to academic issues but would create regular opportunities to discuss their relationship.

### Students expect their supervisors to be constructively critical

This is a particularly sensitive area. It is the supervisor's job to criticize and provide feedback but the manner in which this information is given is absolutely vital. If the criticism is harsh, or perceived as such by the student, untold damage may be done. It is important to remember, also, that giving praise whenever appropriate is one part, often neglected, of providing feedback. During interviews with people who had achieved their PhDs, there were as many unexpected floods of tears (from both men and women) when this topic came up as there were in interviews with those who had dropped out of their PhDs before completing. Doing a PhD is a very emotional, as well as intellectual, experience for most postgraduates.

Yet it is very important indeed that students should have learned how to evaluate their work without recourse to their supervisors by the time they are ready to submit their theses. We have already discussed this in some detail in Chapter 3. It is essential that in the course of discussions with you your students gradually become familiar with the criteria against which their work is being measured. As they become better able to mediate for themselves between their efforts and the results, by comparing what has happened with what they expected would happen, they will need to rely less and less on you for feedback. Relying on their own judgement about their work involves confidence, and this will come only from exposure to continual constructive criticism from a supportive and sensitive supervisor.

If students do not receive helpful information of this sort, there is a high probability that they will become discouraged, lose confidence and decide that they are incapable of ever reaching the standard necessary to do a PhD, which, of course, will affect their future careers. The techniques of giving constructive criticism are discussed later in this chapter.

### Students expect their supervisors to have a good knowledge of the research area

Very often this is the reason that a particular supervisor has been selected. But, especially when students and supervisors have been assigned to each other after registration, it is possible that the supervisor is not expert in the student's area of research. Provided the student has access to others who *are* expert in the area, it may be more important that the supervisor's style of work and expectations of the supervisory role coincide with those of the student.

Students should be able to use other members of the academic staff as a resource. Between them, these academics will probably have the expertise required by the students at different points during the period of research. Alternatively, the strategy adopted by Mrs Briggs and described in Chapter 3 could be used by the supervisor, thus ensuring that students are well catered for by having been introduced to specialists from other universities and polytechnics.

While students consider it essential that supervisors should be well versed in their areas of research, they do not expect their supervisors to be experts on the particular problems they are exploring within those areas. (The reasons for being awarded the PhD degree include an acceptance that the candidate has become an expert on that particular problem.)

There is more to working together than a common interest in an area of research. The relationship between student and supervisor is a dynamic one that is constantly changing. What is important is that communication *about* the research is clear and there is knowledge on both sides of how the work is progressing.

*Students expect their supervisors to structure the situation*
*so that it is relatively easy to exchange ideas*
At first, this expectation appears to be relatively simple. But supervisors find it extremely difficult to achieve. In understanding students, supervisors need to be able to draw out their ideas. They should have the flexibility to understand what the students are trying to say. This is done through continual questioning. Students may speak or write in a convoluted manner from a fear that their thinking will otherwise be considered too simple. They may not yet have managed to clarify their thoughts.

We are not suggesting that supervisors need to take a course in thought-reading. They may, however, need to learn some simple techniques for eliciting information from people who cannot express themselves coherently.

Creating a comfortable environment in which to discuss ideas and so further the research is not an easy task. We have already seen that there is a discrepancy between students' and supervisors' perceptions of degree of familiarity and approachableness. When a supervisor has several research students, a solution might be the introduction of research seminars in which all of them meet to discuss their research with the supervisor present.

If, on the other hand, a supervisor has only one or two students, the department should arrange the seminars and the supervisors should take it in turn to be at them. The presence of one member of staff is necessary to ensure that the seminar takes place but if several are participating, students are often inhibited and less likely to speak up. Gradually, the seminars should help the students to feel freer to discuss their research in tutorials with their supervisors. One option that we do *not* recommend is for one supervisor to take departmental responsibility for the seminars, as many students will then not be able to use the seminar to get to know their own supervisors better.

These seminars provide a training ground invaluable for developing thinking through discussion, helping students to structure their ideas into a form that facilitates writing. They also enable students to practise the skills necessary for presenting their work at conferences.

*Students expect their supervisors to have the courtesy not to conduct a telephone conversation during a tutorial*
This is not an unreasonable request, but it is always greeted with laughter when it is put to groups of supervisors. Setting aside a period to discuss progress makes students feel that they are being taken seriously and conveys the impression that the work under discussion has sufficient merit to be treated with respect. There is nothing more frustrating than to be interrupted in midstream when trying to explain a complex and as yet unexpressed idea. Equally, if student and supervisor are engaged in an intense discussion of a specific issue, the line of thought is difficult to regain. If there are several interruptions the student feels insulted and the work becomes devalued. Any progress that might have been made in creating a comfortable environment is sure to be lost.

During tutorials supervisors should arrange for telephone calls to be intercepted if at all possible. If this is not possible they should tell the caller that they are engaged in an important meeting and will call back. It is just bad manners to permit any but the most urgent call to intrude into a meeting that has been arranged and for which work has been prepared.

*Students expect their supervisors to have sufficient interest
in their research to put more information in the students'
path*

There is a variety of ways in which this can be done. It is important that the supervisor takes into consideration the student's
current need for help. For example, in the beginning it may not
be sufficient to suggest a reference, leaving the student to follow
it up in the library. For some students it may be necessary to give
an actual photocopy of the article if it is difficult to obtain in order
to get them started. Supervisors can also show their students
articles and sections of books from their own collections which
are relevant to the point the student has reached.

At a later stage, conference papers reporting the newest
developments in the field need to be brought to the student's
attention. At this stage the student and the supervisor should
both be reading the relevant literature and sending journal
articles to each other. In fact, the exchange of papers should be
seen as an essential aspect of communication and a source of discussion.

Finally, as we have said, supervisors have a responsibility to
introduce their students to others in the field. These specialists
should be able to give the students more information than the
supervisor alone. Such contacts are important for budding professionals, enabling them to build up a network within which
they can discuss their research interests.

*Students expect supervisors to be sufficiently involved in
their success to help them get a good job at the end of it all!*

This expectation is becoming more and more important each
year as it gets more and more difficult for supervisors to do anything about it. There are some students who decide it is worthwhile to have an 'absent' supervisor for the period of their
research in order to be assured of a good job at the end of it. They
are willing to be supervised by busy, jet-setting academics, even
though they know that they will be left alone for long periods
since their supervisors will be difficult to contact. Research
students assume that their supervisor will be able to effect intro-
ductions to others, of all nationalities, who are also at the top of
their profession. They decide that to have a personal reference
from such a well-known authority is worth three years of isolation in learning to do research.

At all levels of the academic ladder there are those who agree
that it is part of the supervisor's role to help students to find a job

once they have completed. Equally, there are those who consider that a supervisor's tasks are at an end when a PhD degree is awarded. Whichever camp a supervisor may fall into, it may not make very much difference in times when government funding of research is cut and academic employment in general is reduced.

## Establishing a role model

This is a very important aspect of your task as supervisor. It is not a case of saying 'do as I tell you' but more a case of students gradually learning to 'do as you do', whether that is what you would prefer or not. The way you conduct yourself in your dealings with your postgraduate students is therefore vital to their later development. It is crucial for them to see that research is important to you and that you treat it seriously. Nothing could be better for them than your being deeply involved in your own research and writing papers about it that get published in reputable journals. Giving conference papers and attending seminars in your specialized area are activities that benefit your students as well as yourself, without either you or them necessarily being aware of it. What it all adds up to is giving potential researchers a mode of behaviour toward which they can aim.

When you postpone a meeting with a postgraduate because of pressure of other work, such as administration or marking examination scripts, it suggests to the student that those areas of your work take precedence over research supervision. Similarly, if your priorities are orientated to undergraduate lecturing, postgraduates will soon understand that doctoral supervision has a low rating on your long list of responsibilities.

As we are not currently taught how to supervise it is not unrealistic to assume that the next generation of supervisors will treat their PhD students in a similar way to that in which they themselves were treated. Bad supervision breeds bad supervision and postgraduates will continue to feel neglected and depressed. If, on the other hand, today's supervisors act conscientiously in this part of their work, we will have a more contented group of postgraduates who will probably be more successful in their future academic careers. We will also have sown the seeds for future generations of academics to reap the benefits that come from having good role models doing serious work.

## Teaching the craft of research

In general, supervisors do not know how to *teach* how to do research, even though their own research practice may be outstanding. They do not even think of supervision as being a part of their teaching role. Yet it is as important to give some thought to the teaching component in supervision as it is to the research component.

### *Giving constructive criticism*

Giving criticism is one of the main activities that supervisors of postgraduate students have to undertake. We have considered in Chapter 8 the negative effects on students of supervisors who cannot handle this aspect of supervision effectively. It is vital that criticism be given in a constructive and supportive fashion.

Apart from being specific about what precisely is wrong with the student's performance, it is also necessary to know what kind of criticism is appropriate at a given point in the student's research career. For example, a detailed critique of grammar and punctuation will not be of very much use if the ideas and general content of a piece of writing are incorrect or confused.

When discussing progress it is vital that you are very specific about what it is that is required. Merely saying that, for example, you are disappointed that things are going so slowly is no help at all. Instead, you could tell the student that when an unavoidable delay occurs, which prevents the carrying out of an experiment or an interview, for example, he or she should not just stop working. It is necessary to set the wheels in motion to resolve the problem and to continue with some other work such as reading, writing or analysing what has already been done. At the same time a regular check can be kept on developments relating to the removal of the obstacle. The student needs to be *told* all this.

Again, if you hand back a piece of written work saying that it should be rewritten, the student needs to know *what to do*. Should the work be longer or shorter, contain more references to published work, have less complex sentences, contain simpler ideas, use less jargon? Or is it merely the punctuation and grammar that need correction. No matter how obvious it may seem to you, it is essential that you spell out to the student, in very precise terms, just what it is that needs to be redone and why. If all of it needs to be reworked, give explicit advice concerning how the new version must differ from the previous one. It is primarily in this way that students can discover what it is they should be watching for in their own work and so become better at judging what is acceptable and appropriate.

The reason for giving criticism effectively is that through it students can eventually learn how to evaluate their own work and so take over this part of the supervisor's job themselves. In the longer term, they have to be taught how to become independent researchers in their own right.

Supervising a candidate for a PhD involves more than just monitoring the work. Doing a PhD is a very emotional experience, which involves the whole person. As supervisor you need to be able to communicate with your students about their abilities and achievements, but you also need to discuss their commitment to the PhD and any external circumstances that affect it. Throughout their registration period it is highly probable that you will need to take account of their personal lives.

In fact this is true of anybody engaged in supervising another human being, but unfortunately it is too often the case that managers choose to ignore the 'whole person' and patch over, rather than get to the bottom of, any difficulties that are showing themselves in the individual's work. While this is true of life at work in general it is even more true of life within the academic community. Managers do, at least, have some management training during their careers; often these courses contain elements of interpersonal skills and human relations training. Academics rarely have such training opportunities. Yet research students are emotionally more involved with their work than are most people who are responsible to a manager.

Skill in giving constructive criticism and eliciting information that may be relevant to poor performance at work is therefore even more important in the student–supervisor relationship than in the manager–subordinate relationship. However, there is much less likelihood of finding those skills within the academic community. What is needed here is training in how to state honestly and directly what you as supervisor perceive to be the problem, no matter how upsetting you think this may be for the student. It is far worse for the student to think for a long time that everything is reasonably satisfactory, only to discover at a very late stage that the work is not suitable for writing up, or that the thesis will be entered only for an MPhil after all. Alternatively, the student may be aware that things are not as they should be but will imagine all kinds of causes for the problem, including a sudden and inexplicable antipathy on the part of the supervisor.

It is far preferable for the student to have some definite information upon which to base decisions about future behaviour
than to worry that something isn't quite right without knowing
why.

For example, Charles, studying astronomy, wanted to know
whether or not to continue. He said:

> I'd like to if I possibly could, but if Dr Chadwick thought I
> wasn't capable of it I wouldn't be too upset as long as he
> *told* me. Nobody seems to want to advise me.

Dr Chadwick was disappointed with his student's slow progress
and lack of initiative. He said

> He's probably not very organized in his work, although
> one would hope there's some wider reading going on.

However, Charles had reported:

> I asked him if he knew of any review articles but he doesn't
> think there are any. He was busy marking exam papers, so
> we didn't talk . . . I still haven't learned how to communi-
> cate with Dr Chadwick. There's no rapport between us,
> none at all. I saw him in the lift accidentally on the last day
> of last term and all we said was 'hello'.

On the other hand Adam, studying architecture, reported at
the very end of his time as a research student:

> My supervisor never gave me any indication of what he
> thought of me. I decided that he was so bored with what I
> wrote that he couldn't be bothered to criticize what I did.
> But really he was hoping that I would be the one to popular-
> ize the theories that have been around in his department for
> some years.

Adam had not enjoyed his years as a research student but was
feeling much better as the end came into view and he had some
measure of success at a conference. Professor Andrews explained
how the situation had eventually been clarified: 'We had several
discussions about the direction his work was taking.' It is sad that
this only happened once Adam had received support for his ideas
from others, who actually did consider them to be quite excellent.

These two examples are typical of the situations that develop
when supervisors do not keep students informed of how they
see their progress through (a) regular meetings and (b) honest
feedback regarding their work.

Assertiveness training courses (Dickson 1982; Paul 1983) – currently in vogue for the training of women – contain large sections on the giving and receiving of criticism. It might be a good idea for supervisors who feel that they have difficulty with this part of their work to go on one of these courses.

### Introducing a structured 'weaning' programme

In Chapter 7 we described how supervisors can help postgraduates become academically independent by introducing a process of weaning into their style of supervision. In addition to the structure already suggested, this weaning process must include helping the postgraduates to become aware that they have sufficient knowledge and ability to trust their own judgement and monitor their own performance.

With regard to conference papers, journal articles, seminar presentations, thesis chapters or even reports of work undertaken since the last tutorial meeting, a way to get to this point is to encourage the following activities:

- First: the student prepares a rough written draft that sets out 'This is what I think'; then he or she corrects and rewrites the draft without referring to you.
- Next: after discussing the first corrected draft with you, the student prepares a second corrected draft that sets out 'This is what I and my supervisor think'. Then the student can again give the draft to you for comment.
- Finally: the student prepares a final draft that states 'This is it', and may keep it as a record. At the end, all well written records can be used and integrated into the thesis itself.

The way to encourage students to use their supervisors to best advantage is to set goals that initially are short-term but become more abstract and take longer to reach as the student becomes more experienced and develops more confidence.

In Chapter 7 we described in some detail the setting of goals within a time management programme. It is important for you, as supervisor, to be aware that the length of time that it takes for research students to become autonomous researchers depends on the type of supervision that they receive. If they are continually set very short-term goals with the requirement that they complete a relatively simple piece of work, they will never learn how to manage their time, tasks and deadlines for themselves. But, if they are left to their own devices too early, or given deadlines that are too far into the future before they are ready for this degree of unstructured planning, then they will not learn how to cope on their own.

Supervisors must adjust the way they supervise to the particular needs of individual students. Some students will take a relatively long time to develop the necessary confidence. They will need to be closely monitored and given well defined tasks to be completed in a relatively short period, until they are quite well established in their research. Other students will need to be given general guidance, from quite early on, in what they should be doing rather than detailed direction.

One student requiring guidance early on was Greg, who was researching in ancient history. Dr Green explained that Greg

> usually suggests the meetings, but once last term I was con-
> cerned about him and asked to see him. I didn't have to chase him. I just make a passing reference or suggestion and next time I see him he knows the text better than I do. He works extremely well.

She saw her role as that of guide, not only because Greg was able to work well under his own direction but also because he was fascinated by the information he was accruing about the person he was researching and the times in which he lived. Every bit of additional knowledge served to motivate Greg to explore further. His main request of his supervisor was that she be ready to listen to the results of his latest detective work.

A possible paradigm for a structured weaning process in your overall supervision could be:

- *Early direction*. The supervisor introduces short-term goals, sets the work to be done, and gives detailed feedback to the student at the end of the period.
- *Intermediate weaning*. This phase involves support and guidance rather than direction. The work is discussed with the student, and joint decisions are made about what should be attempted and how long it should take. The supervisor encourages the student to evaluate any work submitted and comments on the evaluation, rather than on the work itself.
- *Later separation*. This phase includes an exchange of ideas: the student decides on the work to be done and its time limits. By now the supervisor should expect a detailed critical analysis of the work from the student without prompting.

The timing of these stages will vary according to the developing self-confidence of the students. The main requirement here is that supervisors should recognize the stage that students have reached in their need for support. Supervisors might aim to raise their own level of awareness of students' needs for feedback on their progress. Supervisors also need to teach students, by example, how academics evaluate the results of their own work and use this evaluation as a basis for revision and improvement.

This might be achieved by discussing with their students how the work they have already done affects their plans for further work. In addition, by making explicit the interaction between what they plan to do and what they have already done, supervisors can teach their students to be more cautious and not to get carried away with overambitious projects. Supervisors who are sensitive to the needs of their students and able to teach them to become self-supervising at their own pace will derive greater satisfaction from this part of their work than those supervisors who treat all their students in the same way.

Once students have learned the skills and acquired the confidence necessary to assess their own efforts, their dependence on you as supervisor begins to be superseded by self-reliance. It is at this point that they begin to perceive you not as a tutor but as a colleague.

## Maintaining a helpful psychological 'contract'

Cast your mind back to the start of this chapter and you will recall that Freddy did not discuss with his supervisor how to conduct the research or to what extent and how often Professor Forsdike should be kept informed of results. In this case the professor's behaviour was depressing Freddy and having an adverse effect on his work. They never discussed this problem, and the situation continued without change for most of the time that Freddy was working toward his PhD. Yet it was so easily avoidable; all they had to do was to talk to each other about the context as well as the content of Freddy's work.

A similar lack of communication existed between Adam and Professor Andrews. If Adam had assumed that his supervisor had read the paper (even though privately he believed this not to be the case) he could have asked why Professor Andrews had not bothered to mention more than a small section of it. The conversation would have been opened up enough for the professor to convey his knowledge of the content and express his doubts about the scope of what Adam had done. Such questions from Adam, asked in a positive manner, would have changed their relationship completely. Professor Andrews would have been more expansive in his comments, and Adam would not have spent most of his postgraduate years believing that he was almost totally unsupervised. Of course, if Professor Andrews had put even minimal written comments on the draft, the student would have known that it had been read. Putting a tick at the bottom of each page as you finish reading it will inform your student that nothing has been missed.

It is so easy for postgraduates to become discouraged that a significant part of your job as supervisor is one of keeping morale at a reasonable level. The process of learning to do research and become a full professional involves periods of doubt and disillusionment, when it seems that the only thing to do is to give up. There are periods when moods are volatile, and a certain subtlety is needed to help a student through the difficult times.

Do not be taken in by rationalizations no matter how persuasive they may be. It is not helpful to concede that there is 'no need' for a meeting just now or to forego some evidence of work in progress, because you feel sorry for the student. Of course, you should be supportive when support is needed. But when you discover that there are continually new and ever more important reasons why the student should be given more time, you will need to be firm if the student is not to fall by the wayside.

If there is a good reason for a year's break, then set it out formally as a break within the institutional framework. This will be more helpful in the long term than building up increasing gaps in work on an informal basis. It is damaging to the 'contract' between you for the student to live with uncertainty or lack of constraints. Therefore, it is essential that, at regular intervals, you:

- offer a statement of your expectations, within the oral contract that has already been agreed;
- ask your students what their expectations are;
- agree a compromise incorporating any changes.

Handling the situation in this way would ensure that the student felt the supervisor was neither uncaring nor lacking in control. It would underline the fact that the supervisor and the student are in a partnership.

In order to maintain the psychological contract at an appropriate level it is important that you play your role as supervisor in a firm way. If you let your professional judgement be swayed from a fear of seeming to be too tough at a time of difficulty in a postgraduate's career, you will not be providing help at a time when it is most needed. But the help you need to provide is to chart a course for the student, avoiding the extremes of, on the one hand, easing the path completely and, on the other, leaving the student to founder, simply so that you might appear more sympathetic. It is not your sympathy that the student needs but your expertise.

### Encouraging students' academic role development

It is not sufficient for a supervisor merely to ensure that postgraduates' research and their reporting of it are progressing satisfactorily. As PhD students get closer to the goal of gaining the research degree, so too do they get closer to recognition as a full professional. But becoming a full professional means more than having completed a research project to a satisfactory standard: it means being able to contribute fully to academic life. It is part of the supervisor's job to help students prepare for this.

This entails encouraging your students to give seminars on their research and related topics and to attend seminars that others are giving. It means helping them gain the confidence to question and comment on what has been presented by the speaker. Postgraduates should also gain experience of attending conferences, speaking from the floor (as they have learned to do in seminars) and giving papers of their own.

These papers may be of an appropriate standard for publication, in which case you, as the supervisor, must initiate the students into the secrets of getting their work published in reputable journals. You could give them a helping hand, too, by introducing them to your own network of contacts and encouraging them to get in touch with colleagues who are working in their area of interest. In addition, you should faciliate their progression into academic life by trying to give them occasional tutoring work and letting them know when further teaching possibilities are offered – for example, a weekend or summer school post.

Giving such support to your postgraduate students will not in fact take up very much of your time and energy. When there is a conference you want to go to, all you have to do is mention it to your students and perhaps sign an official request for help with their expenses. Similarly, inviting them to lunch with you once or twice when you are meeting a friend from another university does not make much of a demand on you, yet it has dividends for the students out of all proportion to the effort needed.

In conclusion, we may reflect on what would constitute a satisfying result of good supervisory practice for both the student and the supervisor. Such an outcome would include:

- a doctorate of quality completed on time;
- a paper published in an academic journal;
- a paper presented at an international conference, so that the student has faced external criticism;
- meeting other professionals and arguing with and impressing them, so that they may be used as possible additional referees;
- advancing the topic as a result of the research;
- a stimulating experience for both the student and the supervisor.

If you give just a little of your time to thinking about helping your students to get a foot on the academic ladder, you will be rewarded by having students who not only like and admire you but also will in later years make you proud to acknowledge that at one time you were their supervisor.

## Action summary

1 Be aware of the expectations which students have of supervisors and try to fulfil them. If you are not able to fulfil some of them, or think them inappropriate, do not simply neglect them. Raise them as issues for discussion with your students.
2 Be aware that you inevitably act as a role model for research students. In this respect, the most important single contribution that you can make to their success is to demonstrate continually that you take research seriously in your own academic life.
3 Be aware that supervision, like undergraduate teaching, has to be considered as an educational process and thought must be given to the most appropriate teaching approaches. Look for ways of designing learning situations for the student and improving your ability to give constructive criticism.
4 Since students can easily become discouraged, a significant part of a supervisor's task is keeping their morale high. It is

important to demonstrate that you understand their problems, emotional as well as intellectual.

5 Set up a helpful climate in which there are outline agreements on what the student and the supervisor have to do. If progress is not being made, do not let the position slide. Review the agreements in discussion and renegotiate them if necessary.

6 Look for ways of supporting your research students in their academic careers – for example, by arranging for them to give departmental seminars, present conference papers, discuss their research with leading academics from other institutions, write joint papers for submission to journals, etc.

# 10

# The formal procedures

Each university has a plethora of its own formal procedures concerned with the award of the PhD degree. Polytechnics and other colleges use the CNAA system. You will need to conform with the particular rules that apply to your case. Hopefully, you will have sufficient regular informal guidance from your supervisor, the appropriate section of the academic registrar's department, and so on to keep you away from possible pitfalls. But as with all else in the PhD process, in the end it is your own responsibility to see that you conform to the system.

The purpose of this chapter is to make you aware of some of the key points at which the formal system is likely to impinge on you. We can only do this in general terms, since as we have said, the details vary in different institutions. *You must study the particular regulations that apply to you.*

## Registration

The first question here is: do you have the academic qualifications to be accepted as a student for a research degree? Most universities require first- or upper second-class honours in a relevant British undergraduate degree; some universities will accept lower seconds, as does the CNAA. If you already have a master's degree it is usually acceptable, whatever the class of your undergraduate degree.

These are the general requirements which will allow you to go through straightforwardly. If you do not have them it does not mean that you will not be accepted, only that a special case has to be made, which will require the strong backing of your potential supervisor. For example, if you do not have a British degree, the university or the CNAA will have to satisfy itself that your overseas degree is of a standard equivalent to a British one. Or you may have a non-degree professional qualification plus considerable practical experience, on which a special case could be made for your acceptance.

In general we would say that you should not be immediately deterred if you do not have the typical formal qualifications for acceptance. Always explore with potential supervisors whether a special case can be made. It may be, for example, that you could be accepted subject to doing certain extra study, or passing a qualifying examination. Remember too that if one institution rejects you, it does not mean that all will. However, if you have had more than one rejection it may not be wise to pursue registration. You may need to review your likelihood of success and come to a more realistic estimate of your abilities.

The second question is: what degree are you going to be registered for? If you do not already have an MPhil [i.e. a Master's degree awarded for research] the typical system now is for beginners to be considered as general research students. The decision on formal registration for the PhD is taken after the first year when there is some indication that the work is progressing appropriately. You and your supervisor must, therefore, be in close contact to ensure that the case can be made for full PhD registration. At this stage a title for the thesis and the intended programme of research are presented.

The third question is concerned with the limits of the period allowed between registration and submission. For full-time students there will be a formal minimum time (two years or three years) and, in many institutions now, a formal maximum (eight years, ten years) after which registration will lapse and a special (and very persuasive) case will need to be made for reinstatement. Because of this maximum limit, if you are having to abandon your research work temporarily but intend to return to it, you should obtain a formal suspension of the period of study.

For part-time students the time limits are set roughly *pro rata*: four to five years minimum, ten years maximum. Don't forget that if you are employed by your institution as, say, a research assistant, you may find that you can be counted as a full-time student even if you are working only part-time on your PhD. If you have been following us this far, you will know immediately why this fudge is allowed. It is because the basic nature of the PhD is as a professional training, and research assistants get a great deal of this training as part of their jobs.

When registration has been completed you should be informed formally of: (i) your supervisor(s) (first and second supervisors in the CNAA system); (ii) the topic or field of study for which you have been accepted; (iii) the minimum length of study time required before submission of your thesis.

Continuing registration in succeeding years is usually dependent on adequate progress being made each year, and a report to this effect has to be submitted by your supervisor. Do ensure that it is sent at the appropriate time.

### Grants and research support

It may be that you will qualify for a government grant. The availability of grants is variable, and the regulations on acceptable qualifications detailed. Nevertheless if you are British or have lived in this country for three years or more, it would be worth your while exploring the possibilities. This should be part of your initial discussion with your potential supervisor.

If you are awarded a grant, it will be for a set period (two or three years). Remember that it may be possible to obtain an extension of the grant in some circumstances, and you have to keep your supervisor aware of this possibility and make sure that a strongly supported application is made at the appropriate time. Grants are quite low in value, and it may be that you will be hoping for some casual work. Try to obtain some professional work which helps your academic development if at all possible. It is much better to tutor your subject than to work long hours serving behind a bar.

While academic institutions are no longer regarded as being *in loco parentis*, they may act as quasi-employers if you have a grant that they administer. Some, like any good employer, will make small short-term loans to cover an urgent financial problem. These can be repaid by instalments.

Find out from your university or college what you are statutorily entitled to in the way of research resources. These might include a desk, lab space, equipment and consumable resources (for example, chemicals for your project). You should ensure (via your supervisor, if necessary) that you have them. You also need to be aware that there are often discretionary opportunities available. You may be able to call on technical support from departmental technicians, have your work typed up in a typing pool (inevitably with the lowest priority in the queue, but still . . .) and you may be entitled to apply for travel money to go to conferences or visit other institutions.

## The examination system

This, of course, is the summit of the process, coming as it does at the end of years of hard work. Universities and the CNAA all have their own detailed regulations and you must be well acquainted with those applying to you. But they share a general form, which we shall comment on here.

### Giving notice of submission

You start the whole procedure off by giving notice, usually at least three months beforehand, that you intend to submit your thesis for examination. You should realize that *you* have to make the decision to be examined, in accordance with your professional understanding although you will discuss the matter fully with your supervisor. Formally, you can submit against your supervisor's advice; although this is very risky, it does underline the fact that the decision is yours. It is at this stage that you will normally have to pay the examination fee.

### The appointment of examiners

After you have given notice of submission, the formal procedures are set in motion with the appointment of examiners. The examiners' task is to represent the academic peer group to which you are hoping to gain access. There are several variants of the regulations governing who may be appointed to this role; a key difference is whether your supervisor is allowed to be an examiner or not. In the simplest pattern, your supervisor becomes the internal examiner and one external examiner is appointed. Many universities have this system and it is the normal CNAA procedure. Some universities, though, do not allow your supervisor to be an examiner, and in these cases the internal examiner will be another academic in your department. Sometimes, because of the nature of the thesis topic, there may be two external examiners.

The responsibility for recommending the names of the examiners to the appropriate university or college board is that of your supervisor and head of department. You should expect, though, to be sounded out to give your reactions as to who they might be; and many supervisors, in fact, discuss the issue fully with their students.

It is important for you to know who your examiners are going to be before you actually finish writing your thesis. You should expect that they will be academics whose work you are referring to in your discussion. One rule of thumb is to give first consideration to the British academic whose work is referenced most frequently in the thesis bibliography. But if it turns out that writers quoted in the bibliography are not appropriate, then you must study the works of those who are going to be appointed to see where they can be relevantly quoted. Examiners are only human (you are yourself on your way to being one, remember) and they will certainly expect their work to be appropriately cited and discussed.

## Submitting the thesis

In submitting your thesis there are many rules and regulations to be followed, which vary by institution. There are rules about the maximum length of your thesis, the language in which it must be written (English, unless permission has been previously obtained in special circumstances), the adequacy of its literary style, the size of the pages, the size of the margins, the type and colour of the binding, the number of copies you have to submit, its material state [suitable for deposit and preservation in the library] and so on. You have to be aware of those regulations which apply in your case.

All institutions require the candidate to submit a short abstract, of about 300–500 words, summarizing the work and its findings, in order to orientate the examiners and, later, other readers to the thesis as a whole. You should spend some time on making the abstract cogent, so that it gives a good impression. This is a professional skill that you should develop for both publications and conference papers.

Since, as we have often reiterated, the aim of the PhD is to get you to become a full professional in your field, your examination is not limited to your thesis report, although that is the main way in which you demonstrate your competence. In addition to your thesis you should submit to the examiners as supporting material any academic work to full professional standard that you have already published. Two provisos: the papers must be in the academic field in which you are being examined (you may be a keen philatelist but papers in that field cannot help you if your PhD is in plasma physics); and they must not have been taken into consideration in the award of any other degree of any other institution (you will have to make a declaration to this effect). Joint papers which are relevant may be submitted, and in these cases you have to specify precisely your own individual contribution to them.

### The oral examination – the 'viva'

The oral examination is normally held privately – that is, with only the examiners and the student present. However, some universities allow others to sit in – though not, of course, to take part. (If your university allows it, it is a good idea to watch one beforehand.) Supervisors who are not examiners may be allowed to be present, but usually they cannot take part. In the CNAA system, a non-examining supervisor may, with the consent of the candidate, take part in the discussion, but must withdraw when the examiners consider their decision.

The task of the examiners is to establish that by your thesis work and your performance in the viva you have demonstrated that you are a full professional who should be listened to because you can make a sensible contribution to the development of your field. They are going to argue with you, ask you to justify what you have written in your thesis, and probe for what you see as the developments which should flow from your work.

It can be quite tough because you have got to keep your end up – that is what you get the doctorate for. So you need practice. It is absolutely vital to have had the experience of presenting your work to a professional public beforehand. This 'public' does not have to be big – a couple of academics in your department who are not going to be your examiners but who have had experience of examining would be ideal. Other PhD students should have helped you along the way, as you helped them, and they make excellent mock examiners.

Just as you need practice in writing during your study years if the thesis is to be well written, so you also need practice in public discussion and defence of your work. This is very important, because it is quite appropriate for the examiners to consider, for example, a particular part of your argument in the thesis to be 'thin', but to agree that as a result of your discussion in the viva you have justified it acceptably, and thus the thesis will not be referred back for additional written work on this score.

## The results of the examination

People who have not thought much about the nature of the PhD examination usually believe that candidates will either cover themselves with glory and obtain the PhD immediately or fail and leave in disgrace. This is not so; those are the two extremes of a whole continuum of possible outcomes which we can now consider.

- The PhD will be awarded immediately after the viva. This is the best outcome and the one to aim for.
- The degree will be awarded immediately, but subject to certain corrections and minor amendments, which usually have to be carried out within one month. In effect the examiners say to you: 'If you quickly carry out these changes we will count your revised thesis as the first submission and award the degree.' The changes in this case are usually minor: an incorrect calculation that does not affect the argument, incorrect or inadequate referencing on a particular point, an inadequate explanatory diagram, are examples. You carry out these modifications to the satisfaction of your supervisor/ internal examiner and gain the degree.
- The examiners say 'Yes, but . . .' They think that your thesis and your defence of it are on the right lines but there are weaknesses that must be remedied, and they therefore require you to resubmit it. They will tell you what the weaknesses are, and why, and you will be allowed a certain period – usually up to two years – to complete the work and resubmit it (having to pay, unfortunately, another examination fee). If the examiners have been impressed with your performance at the viva, they do not necessarily have to give you another oral examination on the resubmission.

This result is, of course, very disappointing, but it is very common and should by no means be regarded as catastrophic. Students usually need a couple of weeks to scrape themselves off the floor and put themselves together again, but the best strategy then is to get on with the extra work as soon as possible. After all, if you are in this position you have learned a very great deal from the examination. The examiners will typically specify in very considerable detail what they think is lacking in the work and what should be done about it. Once you get over the emotional frustration, which admittedly can be considerable, you are in a good position to polish off what is required. But don't take too long to get restarted: the emotional blocks can easily cause you to waste the two years. It is a good tactic, both academically and psychologically, to get a paper from your research published in a reputable journal in the intervening period.

Once you have resubmitted and obtained your degree, then of course it doesn't matter – no one will ever know. What matters is what published papers you can get out of the work. You would be surprised at the number of established academics who have had to resubmit their theses.

- The examiners say that the candidate's written thesis was adequate but the defence of it in the viva was not. This is a much less usual result but it underlines the fact that the doctorate is given for professional competence. It is the candidate who passes the degree, not the thesis. If you are in this position you will be asked to re-present yourself for another viva after a certain period (six months to a year), during which you will have read much more widely in your field and gained a better understanding of the implications of your own research study.

   It might also be the case that the examiners decide that your research topic is so narrow that the thesis alone will not give them sufficient opportunity to examine your general professional competence. They can then set you – with due notice, of course – a written or practical examination on the subject area of your thesis work. In that event it is possible that they might regard the thesis as adequate, but require you to resit the examination after a specified period.

- The examiners consider that the candidate's thesis work has not reached the standard required of a doctorate and they do not see any clear way by which it can be brought up to the required standard. However, the work has achieved the lower standard required of an MPhil, and they can award this degree.

   This is a considerable blow; not just because the PhD was not awarded, but principally because the examiners do not see a way of improving it, so it is not likely that the candidate will. It is a result of the candidate (and, we must say, often of the supervisor too) not understanding the nature of a PhD and how to discover and achieve the appropriate standards. The whole burden of this book is to get you to understand and become skilled at the processes of PhD-getting, so that you do not end up in this situation. In our experience most students who are capable of achieving MPhil standard as a consolation prize are capable, in the right circumstances, of obtaining a PhD.

• The examiners may say that the candidate has not satisfied them, and that the standard is such that she or he will not be permitted to resubmit. This is the disaster scenario. It can occur only when the supervisor not only has no conception of what is required for a PhD but does not really understand what research is all about. Of course, it should not occur at all, but it does. However, if the supervisory process and research degree system matched up to anything like the standards we have been discussing in this book, it would not occur. If you did not have the ability to carry out professional research, you would have been counselled on this and advised to leave the system long before getting to the submission stage. You avoid the disaster of failure coming as a bolt from the blue by ensuring that you seek out and learn from those who do know what the process requires.

## The appeals procedures

Most universities now have an academic appeals procedure. The details will vary, and if necessary you must discover what they are for your own institution. They usually enable you to appeal against what you consider to be unwarranted decisions taken against you. For example, under certain circumstances you can be deregistered if the research committee thinks that your work is not progressing satisfactorily, or not progressing at all. You may appeal against this if you provide appropriate evidence, and it will be considered by a subcommittee that contains independent members. The warning note in these cases is always that they would not have occurred if you had not lost contact with your supervisor; and, whatever happens, you must repair this breach or get another supervisor.

Appealing against the results of the examination, particularly when a resubmission is required or an MPhil is awarded, is possible in most universities. It is an option not to be undertaken lightly. You usually have first to demonstrate that your appeal is not 'vexatious', i.e. that you have some *prima facie* argument for your case. The commonest argument is that the examiners were not really expert in the field and therefore used inappropriate standards for judging the work. Obviously that does not come about in any simple way: chemists are not appointed to examine candidates in psychology, for example. But a social historian, say, might feel that the thesis was found inadequate on sociological grounds, because of the bias of the examiners, whereas it should have been considered more as a contribution to history.

That sort of appeal may be considered. The result will be that further examiners are appointed to evaluate the thesis. The problem is that the *more* the examiners, the *less* likely there is to be a favourable result.

Under the CNAA system, appeals against the examiners' decision can be made only on grounds other than those of academic judgement. They can be concerned only with whether the procedures followed in the conduct of the examination were in accordance with CNAA regulations. They are considered by the Council in consultation with the polytechnic.

### Action summary

1 You must obtain and study the regulations of the formal system that apply to you. You should be aware, though, that as a special case, exceptions can be made, and this possibility is often worth exploring.
2 The regulations concern grants, initial registration, adequate progress, doctoral registration, submission of thesis, appointment of examiners, the viva examination, and, in some cases, the appeals procedures. At each point you must ensure that you conform to the requirements.

# 11

# How to survive in a predominantly British, white, male, full-time academic environment

University departments in Britain are largely staffed by British white male full-time academics. In 1983 15 per cent of all academics were women. The majority of these women were in the lower grades as junior research staff, and currently only about two per cent of professors are women. We do not have similar statistics for black academics but it is probable that their representation, in proportion to their numbers in the population, is even lower. Part-time academic staff are also rare in this country. What does this mean for research students who are not members of the majority group?

## Part-time students

What does it mean for part-time students that the PhD process is primarily organized around the idea of three years' full-time work? There are institutions that cater specifically for part-time higher degree students, and there are special arrangements that can be made to do a higher degree on a part-time basis in a conventional university or polytechnic department. However, there are problems experienced by part-time students that the individual engaged in full-time research does not encounter.

The main problem is that of having to switch repeatedly from everyday work to research work. This is primarily a psychological difficulty, but of course time enters into it too. Some students find that trying to work on their PhD every evening after concentrating on other things during the day is self-defeating. It takes so long to get back to where they left off that there is very little time to do any work before needing to get some sleep. Also, once they are absorbed in the task it is just as difficult to force themselves to stop in order to rest.

Part-time students have reported setting aside weekends for their PhD work to overcome these difficulties. The problem then is that they often become resentful at having to give up all their spare time to research and writing. When this happens it is not long before they decide that the work is not worth the effort and begin to change their minds about wanting a higher degree after all.

Another important consideration for part-time postgraduates is the financial side of working towards a higher degree. Usually they are self-supporting, and try to arrange their employment in such a way that they can spend more time on their higher degree work. This might mean that they arrange to work fewer hours for less money over a given period, or take unpaid leave. Without such formal arrangements, they might be tempted to give less value for money at work than they had done previously and find that they are in trouble with their management. All these situations have been described by part-time PhD students during the course of research into the topic over a period of some years.

What all this means is that part-time students are taking on a task that full-timers often find very difficult. Success can come – and is especially meritorious – but you must be prepared to work really hard.

How then to undertake work towards a PhD on a part-time basis with no more than the necessary amount of stress? Here are a few suggestions; hopefully you will be able to come up with some more ideas specifically suited to your own lifestyle, once you have started to think seriously about this situation.

- If at all possible, choose a research problem that is related to your work. As so much of your time is spent in your place of work, it makes good sense to maximize the facilities and resources that are available to you there. In addition, a carefully selected topic can help you to avoid the constant switching that is otherwise necessary for people doing two different jobs.

- Make a contract with yourself to set aside specific periods of time for your PhD work. This might be, for example, alternate weekends and all bank holidays plus two consecutive evenings every week. Or you might prefer to take a whole day once a week or a whole week once a month for uninterrupted work. Whatever you decide, make all necessary domestic and professional arrangements beforehand, so that all the significant people in your life are aware of the way in which you are allocating your time and attention. Having set up a programme that fits into your requirements, see that you stick to it.
- Follow the guidelines laid down in this book for all research students regarding contact with peers, supervisors, academic departments, and research seminars. At the very least regular telephone calls to your supervisor will help to prevent you falling by the wayside.

## Women students

Compared with men of similar ability there are very few women in Britain who continue in education to the level of PhD. They are, therefore, inevitably in a minority in their universities and polytechnics and many find no other female PhD student in their department. Most supervisors are male, and even when there are female supervisors in a department it is not necessarily the case that they will be supervising women. The majority of women postgraduates are, therefore, supervised by men and have little contact with their female peers. Yet these two factors have been shown to be instrumental in discouraging the completion of PhDs by women students.

Lévy (1982), working in America, found that with few exceptions white male students had advantages of academic sponsorship that female students did not. For example:

- going on trips out of state with professors to meet colleagues at other institutions;
- getting paid consulting jobs through the recommendations of their professors;
- getting articles, papers and dissertations typed without personal expense (female students were often asked to type, or at least arrange for the typing, of the professor's work);

● being taken for lunch or a beer with the professor and his friends.

Women students in the United States were less likely to receive such sponsorship from their male supervisors. Yet it has been found that a close relationship with an academic sponsor fosters the development of the appropriate academic self-image. It also provides an essential element in the socialization process of becoming a career academic.

In any large organization much of the important work is done during informal social time. While work can certainly be completed without such social activities, having access to them gives an advantage in terms of being admitted to the 'in' group. There are obvious reasons for female students being treated differently. Many men, even professors, are simply uncomfortable with women and do not know how to communicate with them as equals or even as competent professionals. Their only relationships with women have been those of husband, father, brother or lover in their personal lives, or manager, supervisor or boss in their professional lives. They simply do not know how to play the role of friend or colleague to a woman.

Here in the UK a group of postgraduate students have criticized the paper prepared by the Committee of Vice-Chancellors and Principals on Postgraduate Training and Research (1985) on the grounds that the use of the male pronoun to refer to students, supervisors and heads of departments renders women invisible. They quote the following:

> If at any time the supervisor is of the opinion that the student is unlikely to achieve the degree for which he is registered, he should notify the appropriate authority.

They say that it is such sentences that create difficulties for women, who must work out whether or not they are included in such imagery. Research exists which demonstrates that women do not *feel* included, men do not immediately think of female as well as male images, and children take the words at face value to refer only to men. Documents such as the CVCP's act to exacerbate the special problem women face as research students.

Another group of research students discusses the image of the full-time research student finishing 'his' PhD while 'his' wife types up the thesis, does the housework and raises their children. They say that this is no longer a suitable model on which to base academic facilities and expectations.

Women research students suffer experiences of exclusion as well as isolation. Add to this the fact that a woman student has to cope with paternalism and even sexual harassment in an asymmetrical relationship. There are also problems of 'having to avoid sexual innuendo in order to maintain an amicable, if somewhat uncomfortable, working relationship'.

Stockdale (1986) investigated the incidence of sexual harassment at the London School of Economics. There women make up 38 per cent of the student population, which is about the national average in higher education. Of these, 715 women students, including postgraduate research students, responded to her survey – that is, 51 per cent of the women student population of LSE.

The survey showed that unwanted sexual advances and harassment in the form of personal comments, leers, etc., from both students and members of staff, were a commonplace and widespread problem. A recent National Union of Students survey gave similar results. These findings are also in line with published results of studies undertaken in American institutions of higher education.

The LSE have now appointed an adviser to women students in an attempt to encourage women who have been at the receiving end of unwanted sexual attention to discuss such problems, and possible courses of action, instead of remaining silent.

The scarcity of successful academic role models for women puts them at a further disadvantage when compared to their male peers. In addition, male supervisors of female students may not give feedback as detailed as that which they give to their male students, for fear of the reaction any real criticism might bring forth. If the supervisors believe that women are more emotional than men or feel that they wouldn't know how to cope with tears if they occurred, then once again, the male student is given an advantage denied to his female colleague through no fault of her own. He will know what to do to avoid making the same mistake again, she will not. What can be done to make the situation of female PhD students equal to that of their male colleagues?

First it would help if supervisors – males in particular – were to have some kind of formal training for this part of their job. If they were taught how to give constructive criticism and how to work effectively with women as colleagues and professionals, then a lot of the problems which result from their traditional attitudes would be solved.

Next it is important that you, as a female PhD student, find a peer support group that includes other women. It is not necessary to form a women-only group though. (This is something you may find you want to do in addition.) It would only add to your problems, however, if you joined a peer support group where you were the only woman.

Finally, introduce a supervisor-management strategy that includes telling him directly if you think that you have not been given sufficient information to be able to learn from your tutorial. Ask *what precisely* needs to be done to improve the quality of your work. This strategy must extend to initiating a discussion about the treatment you are receiving if it is unsatisfactory to you. Such a statement will not be easy. But it has to be made immediately you feel the behaviour to be unhelpful – otherwise it will be much worse next time, both in terms of what is experienced and what has to be said. Telling a well-intentioned supervisor that he is being patronizing may not be as hurtful as you think. You need to explain how you feel in a straightforward way that helps him to understand something about his relationship with his female students that he did not know before. Of course, if you are aggressive, matters will be made worse, since he will feel unfairly attacked for trying to be helpful; so do tread carefully.

## Overseas students

In addition to the usual problems experienced by research students, foreign students may feel that they have lost part of their personality by having to express themselves in English all the time. Communication is often a barrier, not only in their academic work but more generally. If you are an overseas student, there is no alternative but to spend time, effort and money in improving your English if it is not up to the required standard. It is a sensible investment that will pay off in the rest of your career, as English is fast becoming the international scientific and academic language.

Even students who come from countries where English is the main language may be surprised to discover that differences in language use cause difficulties in understanding. There is bound to be 'culture shock' – the discovery that accepted ways of behaving vary. The famous English reserve, for example, can be quite discomfiting when you first encounter it.

Accommodation difficulties, financial problems, climatic differences and ill health are further burdens. In addition, overseas students encounter problems in coping with shopping, going to the launderette and negotiating with unfamiliar bureaucracies. Sometimes worries about their families and friends, caught up in political unrest in their home countries, add to the strain.

For overseas students from most other cultures [except North America] the self-starting nature of the British postgraduate educational process may present particular problems. If you come from a culture which accords deference to elders, teachers and seniors of every kind, you will be more used to waiting to be told what to do before starting on a task. At the very least you will expect to get approval for your idea before working on it.

You may come from an educational system which is built on the view that knowledge and wisdom come from the ancients; and that the older a source is, the more senior in status a person is, the more valuable his pronouncements are held to be. You do not argue with your father, your guru, your professor: that would be showing disrespect. You are here to learn from your supervisor by doing what you are told.

If you hold this view you will have to work very hard to understand the nature of the new culture that you are entering. First, it is a scientific and academic culture that values novelty and change. Everybody is striving for new conceptions, new analyses, new results which give more knowledge, more understanding, more insight, more control. Older approaches are superseded and become of historical interest only. Newton is still regarded by many as the greatest physicist who ever lived, but we no longer study his works in modern physics. We do not regard it as a paradox that we know more about the English Civil War than historians did a century ago, although they were living considerably nearer to it.

Secondly, it is a culture in which you are being prepared to play your role as a partner in this process. You are being helped to think for yourself, take initiatives, argue with your seniors and so on, in order to demonstrate that you have something to contribute to the continually changing academic debate.

Thirdly, to help you on in this you will be left to your own devices for much of the time, and this is regarded as an opportunity, not as a deficiency.

This culture difference becomes extremely debilitating, if it is not conquered, by the time you get to the end of your period of research and have to face the oral examination. In this situation the student is expected to provide an assertive and confident defence of the thesis. It could happen that students who had been taught in their home cultures to be respectful to those in authority would find it far more difficult to engage in any real argument with an examiner. The examiner would have a high status and probably be older than the candidate, thus making a discussion between equals almost impossible for the overseas student.

Overall then, you must realize that it takes a significant amount of time for *any* new research student to settle in and begin useful work. Because of these additional difficulties, you must not become impatient if it takes rather longer for you.

Some suggestions for tackling these problems include:

- finding out as much as possible about Britain before coming;
- developing a support network of both new and experienced overseas students;
- using university societies where people from your home country can meet to help minimize the shock of accommodating to the new culture;
- getting to know non-university compatriots for social activities, particularly if these are not to be found at the university;
- observing, in the first instance, and eventually participating in situations where the usual criticism, challenge and debate take place, to familiarize yourself with this non-deferential activity as an accepted part of the academic process;
- attending a course on assertiveness skills to get to the point where you feel confident enough to participate in the academic process.

## Ethnic minorities

There are differences here between those students who come to study in British universities from overseas and those whose home is in Britain. Nevertheless, students who are members of ethnic minority groups still have problems that are specifically related to that fact, whether or not they are working in what is, for them, a second language.

Levy (1982) cites the case of a black student in the United States who was accused of not having written her thesis unaided and was made to prove that it was in fact independent work, because her professor believed that blacks in general cannot write. There has been no similar research in Britain, so we do not know whether there are academics in British universities who consciously treat their black students differently from their white students in such a way. What we do know is that black students are conspicuous by their absence from this level of education in this country. It seems to be the case that if discrimination does occur, it occurs at the point of entry into the system.

Winston, an Afro-Caribbean student educated in this country, spoke of the lack of role models for disadvantaged groups. He said that one of his main reasons for wanting the doctorate was to demonstrate to other black students that it *was* possible.

Carina, a black student researching minority cultures, told of difficulties in gaining entry to a university department at research degree level. She described becoming a research student as a closed shop and repeatedly spoke of exclusion and exclusivity. Carina said that when talking to potential supervisors she had been told that:

- black research on minority cultures is biased, and therefore whites do it better;
- it has all been done already; we know everything there is to know about the black minority in this country.

She explained that, as an act of self-preservation, students from ethnic minority groups select the institutions to which they will apply very carefully indeed. They have to know the university and the attitude of its academic staff very well before they will put themselves into the position of even being considered. Also, she reported that she and her non-white friends had got used to being subjected continuously to administrative bureaucracy, such as being asked for identification whenever they went into the library, whereas white students were allowed in on the nod.

Ways in which you can help to overcome problems directly related to discrimination include:

- Take time to discover the attitudes of members of staff when choosing the institution for your research work. Gauge that you are able to cope with the level of prejudice that you may expect to find.
- Set up a peer support group of other, similar students – across colleges or institutions if necessary.
- Use 'assertion techniques' to introduce the topic of discrimination with the person most directly concerned, immediately you feel it to be necessary.
- Contact your NUS representative for help if you think that you need formal support for a specific grievance.

## Action summary

The overall message for all these groups is to get what social support you can for your disadvantaged interests.

For part-time students:

1 Choose a research problem that is related to your work.
2 Set aside regular specific periods of time for your PhD work and stick to them.
3 Keep in regular contact with supervisors, peers and the department. At the very least make regular telephone calls on your progress.

For women students:

1 Join or establish a peer support group that includes other women.
2 Discuss with your male supervisor any problems in the male/female aspect of the student/supervisor relationship.
3 Use assertion techniques in tutorials in order to get *precise* information about how to improve your work.
4 Use the NUS to influence your college to appoint a women's officer and to establish procedures to deal quickly and fairly with complaints regarding harassment.

For overseas students:

1 Find out as much as possible about Britain and the British educational system before coming, and during your early period here.
2 Join or establish a support network of both new and experienced overseas students.

For students from ethnic minorities:

1 Join or establish a peer support group.
2 Use assertion techniques in situations in which you are not being treated comparably with other (white) students.
3 Whenever necessary enlist the help of your NUS representative or a member of staff, possibly from another department, to whom you can explain your experience of unfair treatment.

# 12

# The limitations of the

# present system

The PhD system is under considerable pressure at present, both financially and educationally. Financially, there are greater difficulties in getting adequate resources for research work and research students. Educationally, the concept of a PhD and the processes involved in obtaining it are being questioned, and new formulations proposed. In this chapter we shall discuss a number of major issues which are the focus of debate.

**Who should be eligible to embark on a PhD degree?**

All that we know about selection is that we do not know how to select research students who will be successful. Hudson (1960, 1977a) and Miller (1970) discuss the poor predictive quality of final undergraduate examination results and call for research into this level of education. Whitehand (1966) recommends tests of problem-solving, rather than knowledge, for selection of research students.

Even though this has been a topic of discussion for more than a quarter of a century, little or nothing has been done about it. We still select people who have performed well in undergraduate exams and reject those who have the enthusiasm, determination and persistence to apply themselves to research, just because they have not managed to achieve at least an upper second in their degree. That is an arbitrary requirement set up by research councils and universities, yet even experienced supervisors have difficulty in specifying the embryonic qualities that will gradually develop into the mature characteristics of a successful research worker.

New postgraduates have spent long years at school receiving knowledge that helped them to pass examinations. It is probable that their undergraduate courses were also based on a model which resulted in the handing out, as opposed to seeking out, of information. Snyder (1967) noted that, at the undergraduate level in science and engineering, very bright students were always asking questions. These students were often regarded by the staff as a nuisance. This means that those qualities most likely to be needed for a researcher, namely curiosity and the ability to see different possibilities in a situation, may be precisely those that are discouraged in the population from which research students are drawn. Further, the very students most suited to research are those who have had more negative experiences with members of the academic staff. It is these students who would be most likely to lose interest in their work at undergraduate level and therefore not perform well in exams. Even if they did get the required class of degree they would be less likely, because of their experiences, to be tempted to apply for a place on a higher degree course. Of course, some undergraduates may be lucky in having lecturers who are stimulated by novelty and dissent, but this is by no means general.

The approach to higher education based on the handing out of information is merely a continuation of what occurs at an earlier age. De Bono (1973), for example, demonstrates that at the end of long years of formal education there is a deterioration in the thinking ability of children, which is reflected in their attempts to solve problems. He shares Bruner's (1972) view that schooling in our society not only makes it unnecessary for the learner to think, but also makes it difficult for the pupil who proposes an unacceptable, new point of view. Bruner describes the process of the reduction to a minimum of fantasy, imagination and clever guessing. Yet these are precisely the qualities that are needed to do good research.

We therefore maintain that it has already been too long since entry criteria have been seriously reconsidered by the research councils and universities. This should be given top priority. Instead of taking degree classification as the *only* indicator of research potential, we suggest that, at a minimum, weight should be given to performance in undergraduate student projects. In addition, tests of problem-solving and flexible thinking, along the lines of those developed by Wason (1960, 1968), should be considered for use in the selection of research students. The aim of such tests is to diagnose the *approach* that the candidate takes to solving the problems set. The correctness of the answer would be of only secondary importance in identifying research potential.

### What training do supervisors need, and how are they to get it?

It is clear that some form of training is needed to help academics to play their role of supervisor more effectively. We take this view as a result of talking to numerous supervisors over a period of many years and participating in discussion groups attended by supervisors from different universities and polytechnics.

Discussion groups can be very helpful for well established and inexperienced supervisors alike. The supervisors should be from different departments (or, better still, from different colleges or universities) so that discussion can focus on the role of the supervisor without being taken over by a hidden agenda of vested interests or political and personal differences.

There is no need for the people taking part to be from the same professional group, since the discussions should focus on the process of doing a PhD and what it means for supervision. We have already stressed the importance of supervisors' being able to discuss other aspects of the relationship with their students and not always focusing narrowly on the content of work in progress.

The activity of the groups needs to be facilitated by an independent professional, such as a counsellor or trainer, with close knowledge of education at this level. There is also a need for a rough structure indicating topics to be discussed during the life of the group. Usually the topics emerge spontaneously as the discussion progresses, but sometimes it is necessary for the facilitator to introduce a topic. However, there is no formal programme or written agenda.

Supervisors are given the opportunity to discuss what each of them considers necessary for good quality supervision at each stage of the research process. This is an aspect of academic work that is not usually discussed, so most people assume that everyone else is doing it well and are embarrassed to talk about any doubts they may have when supervising their own students. At the discussion groups supervisors have the opportunity to discover that most or all of the others are as unsure about what constitutes good supervision as they are themselves.

Topics to be covered should include such things as: 'How to select research students' and 'Problems of supervision'. Questions could be asked about the embryonic qualities required in applicants that could be expected to develop into the characteristics of an able research worker. Participants would be encouraged to discuss frankly the aspects of supervision that bothered them and ask for suggestions from others about how they would overcome such difficulties with their own research students. They might become involved in the question of what it is that the PhD degree is awarded for. Is it for competent work at a high level of specialist knowledge or is it for independent work of a creative nature? The whole area of supervising writing and teaching the skill of evaluating one's own work, might be explored. Eventually the role of an academic supervisor would become much more clearly defined.

## Should teaching credit be given for doctoral supervision?

One important prerequisite for improving supervisory capability is the allocation of teaching credit for doctoral supervision. Traditionally academics have been expected to accept doctoral students as an addition to other duties. They have not been given any teaching compensation for this activity because it was held that the higher status gained by having such students was sufficient reward in itself.

As effective doctoral supervision becomes more and more important in determining whether a department or even a university will be in a position to have doctoral students, this neglect of proper recognition for supervisory duties has increasingly come to be seen as inadequate. In some institutions some credit is now given against administrative or other teaching duties. But it is clear that an appropriate system of credit will have to be devised and applied more generally to all.

Such a development can take place only in the context of a system that attempts to monitor all the work of academics to ensure that the teaching and administrative tasks are distributed fairly. In two such schemes known to us the supervision of a full-time research student counts as one tenth of the academic's teaching load; a part-time student counts as one twentieth.

## Should doctoral programmes be encouraged?

The concept of a doctoral programme comes from the United States. We shall describe its typical structure below, as we attempt to answer the question of whether its adoption would offer advantages over the British system.

The traditional British pattern is of the lone research student supervised by a single academic. The supervisor is responsible for providing all the assistance that the student needs in discipline content, research methodology and topic development, as well as inculcating professional standards and providing personal support. It is quite a tall order, and many supervisors attempt only parts of it. The frequent limitation on the amount of assistance that can be given by one supervisor, coupled with the isolation of the single student, has resulted in low completion rates.

This is clearly unsatisfactory and, at the very minimum, all institutions should adopt a *structured induction procedure* for all newly registered research students. Every new research student should be required to attend a regular series of meetings (fortnightly or monthly) led by a particular member of staff with an interest in and responsibility for postgraduate research. It is important that new students know that there is an identifiable academic who has a major responsibility for them.

The meetings continue over the first six months and cover such topics as what doing a PhD means, the relationship between students and their supervisors, what a thesis looks like, fears and expectations of the research student's role, the importance of working to deadlines – in fact most of the issues with which this book has been concerned. What such a programme achieves is the raising of awareness, *at the very beginning*, of the processes involved in undertaking a three-year period of research training. Students may be told about the different stages through which they can expect to pass. This will not protect them from experiencing boredom, depression and the rest, but at least they will be able to recognize what is happening to them when it does happen and this will be valuable. Other people should be invited to speak to the group about particular topics; they could include a newly successful PhD graduate, an administrator from the registrar's department with responsibility for the formal system, and so on.

Such a series of meetings enables students to identify others in a situation similar to their own and so makes them feel part of a community. It introduces them to the common aspects of being a research student, rather than reinforcing the differences between disciplines and faculties. Finally, it enables them to choose whether they wish to continue meeting as a group, perhaps without any member of staff, to discuss their progress and their problems.

A doctoral programme goes further than an induction procedure and has two key characteristics that attempt to overcome some of the limitations of the lone student supervised by the single academic:

- there are many students, organized by faculty, department or research unit, who combat isolation by providing a support group of peers;
- it provides a common educational core to decrease the teaching load on the supervisor.

The precise content of the core studies needs to be hammered out by each discipline, but to be effective it must be seen by the students as contributing directly to their professional development as researchers and thus to be concerned with skills as well as knowledge. Unlike their counterparts in the American system (explained below), the courses should not be examined. This underlines the fact that their purpose is to help students prepare for their research work, rather than to be an extra formal hurdle to jump.

Exemptions from the courses should be permitted if a good case is made on the basis of previous work. However, no research student should be permitted to proceed to the project work for the PhD degree without first having acquired (whether through an introductory taught course, or prior to registration) a comprehensive knowledge of research methodology and analysis.

The core teaching arrangements should include the induction programme for new students described above, opportunities for students to present seminar papers on their work, and regular discussion of the issues that arise in getting a PhD, of the kind discussed in this book.

The resources required to provide a core teaching component can be made available only if there is a group of research students to receive it. Groups have the added benefit that they enable research students to become an identifiable section of a department. Participants in a programme are thus in a more advantageous position to press for greater recognition of the needs of both research students *and* supervisors. The existence of a doctoral programme makes it easier to obtain physical space and material resources for students, to arrange teaching credit recognition for the work of supervisors and to facilitate changes between supervisors should this become necessary. A programme should have a programme director or departmental research tutor who would monitor the progress of students and be an extra resource to help things along when required. The resulting structure provides a clear framework for students to identify with and from which they can receive social support.

Thus far the general concept of a doctoral programme seems to have many advantages. But there are a number of variants which must be considered separately in further detail. Depending on the structure, programmes can be either very helpful indeed or decidedly unhelpful. We shall consider: (i) the American model; (ii) the scientific research programme; and (iii) the departmental cohort system.

### The American doctoral programme

Doctoral programmes in the United States typically last four years and have this structure:

first year: taking taught courses;
second year: preparing for qualifying examinations;
third year: formulating an acceptable research proposal;
final year: completing the research and writing the dissertation.

The taught courses are very formal and with their enormous emphasis on the methodological inadequacies of previous work run the real risk of knocking any creative thoughts out of the research student.

In the second year students experience very high levels of stress as they prepare for yet another set of examinations, and this is the period during which many students drop out of the programme. For many students it is followed by two years of social isolation, which certainly offer no advantages over the British student's similar three-year experience.

A major difference in the USA is that each student has a thesis committee made up of three members of academic staff, instead of a single supervisor. In practice, the chair of the committee becomes the leading supervisor with all the possible problems that we have been discussing throughout this book. There are, though, two other supervisors who may intervene in the work of the student, often at quite an advanced stage. There are often the problems between colleagues that we have mentioned when discussing joint supervision.

It should be noted that the three members of the thesis committee constitute the examining board, and the degree is awarded if they are satisfied that the student has carried out the approved thesis proposal. There are no external examiners involved, which means that standards vary widely between universities and between disciplines within each university.

In our view, the American system in detail has little to offer British practice, other than the useful concept of the doctoral programme itself.

### The scientific research programme

The doctoral programme that is an adjunct of a major programme of scientific research activity exists in the UK. Research students in such a programme are treated as the most junior level of employee contributing to the overall work, in fact as junior research assistants. The director of the programme sets very clear constraints on the work that is to be carried out and submitted for the doctorate and the student's contribution is correspondingly restricted in range.

Viewed in educational terms, this type of programme has both advantages and limitations. The student's two major advantages over the traditional isolated research student are that the environment continually demonstrates that research *matters* – a great benefit as compared with the situation of students who have supervisors for whom research cannot be the top priority – and the training in professional practice and the academic issues tackled will be 'state-of-the-art'.

These programmes do have limitations, though: first, supervisors tend to discount the necessity for *tutorial* support as distinct from *managerial* supervision, since they believe that much of that support is being given by the group. The close contact that they have with the students in the laboratory on a day-to-day managerial basis leads many supervisors to neglect the educational practices that we have been advocating throughout this book.

Second, directors of research programmes and other senior members tend to accept the illusory picture of teams of happy researchers working together toward a common end. As we have discussed in Chapter 2, this view takes no account of the students' competitiveness and their fear of having their ideas or results stolen by one of their colleagues working on a very closely related problem. The tensions and distrust among such a group of beginning professionals – physically close but psychologically isolated – are very unsettling.

In the view of one of us (EMP), these research programmes should not be encouraged. There are several reasons for this. Once a department adopts such a programme of research it virtually closes its doors to all applications that are not in the specific area that has been selected. For example, if, as was the case in Diana's department, all research grants are given for anti-cancer work, then a biochemist in any other field would have to look elsewhere for a PhD place. Taken to an extreme, a situation could arise in which every research department had only one area of research. The disastrous corollary of this would be that numerous other areas of research would be discarded and, even worse, never begun. The implications of this would be very serious. It would mean that some areas of research were developed on a wide scale, while others were left to the whims of individuals within a few departments, and some were totally neglected.

In DSP's view, the advantages of such programmes in creating a research environment far outweigh their limitations. Yet very real efforts need to be made in them to take cognizance of the 'process' issues discussed in this book. In particular, research directors should take more seriously the fact that their educational responsibilities to their students are distinct from, and additional to, their managerial responsibilities for their programmes.

## The departmental cohort system

A programme based on a PhD cohort within one department is a promising new development. In this case people elect to work in a specific area: for example, stress in alloys (in a department of materials science) or stress at work (in a department of industrial psychology). Within the selected area students define their own problems, which can therefore be quite distinctive and farther apart than in an integrated programme of research as described above. The cohort is led by two members of staff with an interest in the chosen topic area, and these two people act as supervisors to all members of the group until such time as this is no longer appropriate.

The group meets regularly every two weeks, say, to talk about what they are doing. The format is that of a workshop in which one member's progress, problems and thinking are discussed by the staff and other students. They provide feedback, help, information and comparisons from their own experience. In this way there is a constant sharing and exchange of views and the group becomes a support network. In addition, people can discuss problems by telephone, or meet outside the formal group, as they wish.

Early meetings of the cohort cover induction issues; later meetings serve to determine when any member of the cohort needs to be linked to a particular member of staff and so become a more traditional PhD student.

It may be that even after all members of the cohort have been assigned to individual supervisors (and the cohort leaders may act in this capacity) they still wish to meet as a group. The structure and development of the group need to be kept as flexible as possible to accommodate the needs of different cohorts but the format is always the same during the early stages of its life.

In general there is little doubt that the concept of a doctoral programme, flexibly adapted to the needs of particular departments and students, is a most promising way forward, for the reasons listed at the beginning of this section. There are inevitably potential hazards which need to be guarded against in this development, the most formidable of which is the view that PhD students should be trained *only* in doctoral programmes. In our view this would be an unwarranted restriction. Individual students, well supervised, have an important place, if only to set limits to the centralization of research resources ('research selectivity'), which is currently so prevalent.

### Should work for the PhD be a series of projects or a 'big bang' thesis?

A more radical reform of the PhD system, which has been suggested on several occasions (e.g., Halstead 1987) is to encourage moves away from the award of the degree on the basis of *one* piece of research. They argue that the attempt to evaluate academic competence on the basis of a large 'big bang' project is unrealistic – particularly so as it takes place at the initial stages of the researcher's career. At the beginning it would be much more sensible to require the students to demonstrate their range of professional skills through a series of smaller projects. They propose that the PhD should be awarded on the basis of, say, four projects, each of which is carried out to the standards of publishable papers in refereed academic journals.

In our view this is a development which should be encouraged. It fits in well with the approach that we have been putting throughout this book on the professional nature and meaning of a doctorate. For most beginning professional researchers, it would make a much more realistic introduction to the academic work which they can be expected to contribute at the outset of their careers. Useful, publishable academic contributions are more likely to result from such a series of appropriately related studies. Indeed it would not be unrealistic in this approach to require the project papers, or some of them, actually to have been published in reputable journals *before* the degree is awarded. The definition of 'reputable' would be the responsibility of the examiners.

In fact this approach would extend the application of the 'PhD by published work' route which is offered by many universities. Currently this is available to full-time staff only, and without the benefit of supervision. It would, though, fit well into the supervisory framework that we have been advocating. The project approach could with benefit be offered as an optional alternative to the more traditional 'big bang' PhD.

## Should the supervisor be an examiner?

This has been a contentious issue for some years. There are considerable variations in the practices of different universities, with some barring the supervisor from being one of the examiners for the PhD, while others, and the CNAA, *expect* the supervisor to be the internal examiner. Yet other universities allow this but require that if the supervisor is the internal examiner then *two* external examiners must be appointed.

The 1986 CVCP guidelines recommend that 'the candidate's supervisor should be the internal examiner in exceptional circumstances only' (p. 26). It further recommends that 'where the supervisor is exceptionally appointed as internal examiner, a second external examiner should be appointed'.

If the supervisor is not to be an examiner, there is a further debate as to whether he or she should even be present at the viva. There have been different decisions within the same institution, depending upon the terms agreed by particular departments. Some academic boards believe that the student needs to see a familiar face during what may well be experienced as 'quite an ordeal'; some believe that supervisors who have not yet been examiners need to learn how others do it in order to become examiners themselves. Some point out that if the result of the examination is a requirement for a resubmission, then the supervisor must certainly be present to effectively supervise what needs to be done. There are others, though, who believe that it is better for the supervisor to be completely uninvolved in the viva if the student is to be properly and fairly examined.

The main argument against having the supervisor as examiner is that external examiners have often felt that the supervisor is being examined at least as much as the candidate. If supervisors take any academic criticism of the work as an attack on their own professional standards of research, or even if they are thought likely to do so, this acts to inhibit the external examiners from conducting a proper searching evaluation of the thesis.

A related argument has it that if the supervisor even has too much say in the appointment of the external examiner, this can result in the 'I'll scratch your back if you'll scratch mine' syndrome: Here the supervisor of a mediocre student asks a friend to do the examining knowing that the latter will in turn ask the supervisor to become examiner for an equally mediocre student. Neither of these cases, the inhibition or the collusion, is desirable.

Quality needs to be maintained and the aim is that the PhD should be awarded for work of a uniform standard regardless of institution. This is agreed on both sides; the argument is about how this is best achieved.

The arguments in favour of the supervisor being the internal examiner are based on two points. First, examining students whom one has taught is the usual, and appropriate, pattern for university level education (unlike O- and A-levels, for example). With undergradute and taught masters' degree courses it is not regarded as inappropriate that there should be sufficient 'distance' between staff and students to enable the lecturers to set and mark examination papers for their own students – with the participation, of course, of external examiners. And the same position holds for research degrees.

Secondly, being the internal examiner is the mechanism that enables the supervisor to develop this necessary 'distance' during the course of the student's progress – the crucial weaning process that we described in Chapter 9. Because a school examination is set entirely externally, there is nothing to stop a schoolteacher from coaching a pupil right up to the morning of the exam. Non-examining supervisors can fairly argue that it would be perfectly proper to do the same for PhD students, since, like schoolteachers, they are involved only in the tuition, not in the examination itself. It is by making supervisors examiners that we have the institutional mechanism to ensure the proper weaning of student into independent professional.

Of course, it might be argued that some supervisors, even when they are examiners, do not in fact develop this detachment in the later stages of the research. But such cases are due to misunderstandings of the system and can be tackled as such through critical discussion, if the logic of the situation is understood.

The problem of the external examiner being inhibited from making criticism is not one that we have come across. External examiners, in our experience, make very trenchant criticisms of the work if that is justified, even with the supervisor present as a fellow examiner. The collusion problem should be tackled by more careful scrutiny of the proposed examiners in the appropriate university committee, as the CNAA does currently, and, if necessary, by having two external examiners. Although this puts up the cost, both in time and money, of examining a PhD, it is in principle acceptable when we consider that examiners represent the academic discipline when they award the degree. After all, the original concept of a doctorate required it to be defended publicly with the participation of the *whole* university faculty, and this is still the case in some European universities.

## Conclusion

This chapter has addressed some of the issues that we consider vital to the survival of the PhD as a developing system. At a time when academic policy-makers are seriously trying to improve this aspect of higher education, it is crucial that policies be defined which work to the advantage of the whole system. Tinkering with procedures that have been in operation for years will not have any overall or long-term effect. Neither will grafting on practices adopted from other systems, such as those of the USA.

The ideas in this book are all based on systematic study, over many years, of the PhD in operation. Taken as a whole they form the basis of a coherent reappraisal of the system and thus make a contribution to the developments currently being introduced. As well as improving the quality and completion rate of doctorates, these policies would greatly improve the experience that individual students have of actually *doing* a PhD.

# References

Baddeley, A. (1979). 'Is the British PhD system obsolete?' *Bulletin of the British Psychological Society*, 32, 129–131.

Bruner, J. (1972). *The Relevance of Education*. London, Allen and Unwin.

Cohen, D. (1977). *Psychologists on Psychology*. London, Routledge and Kegan Paul.

CVCP (Committee of Vice Chancellors and Principals). (1985; revised edn. 1986). *Code of Practice on Postgraduate Training & Research*.

De Bono, E. (1973). *Children Solve Problems*. London, Penguin Education.

Dickson, A. (1982). *A Woman in Your Own Right: Assertiveness and You*. London, Quartet.

Francis, J. R. D. (1976). 'Supervision and examination of higher degree student's.' *Bulletin of the University of London*, 31, 3–6.

Halstead, B. (1987). 'The PhD system.' *Bulletin of the British Psychological Society*, 40, 99–100.

Hudson, L. (1960). 'Degree class and attainment in scientific research.' *British Journal of Psychology*, 51, 1, 67–73.

Hudson, L. (1977a). 'Picking winners: a case study in the recruitment of research students.' *New Universities Quarterly*, winter, 32, 1, 88–107.

Hudson, L. (1977b). Interview in Cohen (1977) *op. cit.*

Kuhn, T. S. (1970). *The Structure of Scientific Revolutions*. Chicago, University of Chicago Press.

Levy, P. S. (1982). 'Surviving in a predominantly white male institution.' In Vartuli, S. (Ed.) *The PhD Experience: A Woman's Point of View*. New York, Praeger.

Lowenthal, D. and Wason, P. C. (1977). 'Academics and their writing.' *Times Literary Supplement*, 24 June, 781. Reprinted in *Leonardo* (1980), 14, 57.

Medawar, P. B. (1964). 'Is the scientific paper a fraud?' In Edge, D. (Ed.) *Experiment*. London, BBC Publications.

Miller, G. W. (1970). *Success, failure and wastage in higher education*. London, University of London Institute of Education/Harrap.

Murray, D. M. (1978). 'Internal revision: a process of discovery.' In Cooper, C. R. and Odell, L. (Eds) *Research on Composing*. Illinois, NCTE.

Olson, D. (1975). 'The languages of experience: On natural language and formal education.' *Bulletin of the British Psychological Society*, 28, 363–373.

Paul, N. (1983). *The Right to be You*. Bromley, Chartwell-Bratt.

Phillips, E. M. (1979). 'The PhD: Learning to do research.' *Bulletin of the British Psychological Society*, 32, 413–414.

Phillips, E. M. (1980). 'Education for research: The changing constructs of the postgraduate.' *International Journal of Man–Machine Studies*, 13, 1, 39–48. Reprinted in Shaw, M. L. G. (Ed.) *Recent Advances in Personal Construct Technology* (1981). London, Academic Press.

Phillips, E. M. (1984). 'Learning to do research.' *Graduate Management Research*, 2, 1 (autumn), Cranfield School of Management.

Phillips, E. M. (1987). 'What research students expect of their supervisors.' *Hypothesis*, 15, 5–10, University of Bradford Management Centre.

Popper, K. (1972). *The Logic of Scientific Discovery* (3rd edition). London, Hutchinson.

Snow, C. P. (1958). *The Search*. (New ed.) London, Macmillan.

Snyder, B. (1967). '"Creative" students in science and engineering.' *Universities Quarterly*, March, 21, 2, 205–218.

Stockdale, J. E. (1986). 'Sexual harassment in a university setting.' Paper presented at the British Psychological Society Conference, City University, London.

Vartuli, S. (Ed.) (1982). *The PhD Experience: A Woman's Point of View*. New York, Praeger.

Wason, P. C. (1960). 'On the failure to eliminate hypotheses in a conceptual task.' *Quarterly Journal of Experimental Psychology*, 12, 129–40.

Wason, P. C. (1968). 'Reasoning about a rule.' *Quarterly Journal of Experimental Psychology*, 20, 273–81.

Wason, P. C. (1974). 'Notes on the supervision of PhDs.' *Bulletin of the British Psychological Society*, 27, 25–29.

Watson, J. D. (1968). *The Double Helix*. London, Weidenfeld & Nicolson.

Whitehand, J. W. R. (1966). 'The selection of research students.' *Universities Quarterly*, December, 21, 1, 44–48.

# Index